MW01290181

The Spinsterlicious Life

20 Life Lessons for
Living Happily Single and Childfree

Eleanore Wells

THE SPINSTERLICIOUS LIFE.

ACKNOWLEDGMENTS

So many people deserve thanks for helping me along the way on this very exciting venture. Big hugs and deep gratitude to:

- My siblings, Phyllis Wells Blair and Sam Wells, Jr. for loving me and just letting me be me.
- Shannon Mullen for being one of the first to convince me that I really should do this, and showing me how; Tricia Messeroux for pushing me and even holding writing sessions at her house so I didn't slack off; Andy Tuck for being the first to read and critique the earliest draft, and guiding me on making it better.
- Sheila Anderson for her feedback and advice about the industry.
- Faith Childs-my agent and dear friend-who surprised me by loving my book at the first read, then supporting me and guiding me every step along the way.
- Susan Delson (WomensVoicesforChange.org) and Ellen Breslau (Hearst Magazine/Women's Day) for believing in and seeing the value in my story. Bella DePaulo for her activism in the area of singlism…and including me in her book of the same name.
- A whole host of friends who've loved and supported me for years, no matter what I'm doing: Benilde Little (my first real writer friend), Angie Hancock, Cindy Cox Roman, Colleen Branch, Cynthia Stringfield Milanez, Derek Johnson, Karen Williams, Lauren Deleon, Lorraine Wilson-Drake, and Vickie Smith Timberlake.
- The people who appear-by name-in my stories: AJ, Baldwin, Carla, Darlene, Dexter (my nephew), Dillon, Faye, Felicia, Ford, Jackie, Kira, Lori, Lucy, Mau-

reen, Michelle, Nicky, Peter, Pat, Renee, Susan, Traci, Tony, and Vita.

- And those who do not appear by name, for obvious reasons, thanks for providing the stories.
- And the thousands of readers of my blog–TheSpinsterliciousLife.com–who made me laugh, gave me something to think about, and generally helped bolster the "Single Is Ok" movement.

TABLE OF CONTENTS

INTRODUCTION
- So here's the deal -

I am a bit of a serial dater, so over the years many friends have encouraged me to chronicle some of my adventures in dating—even though most of my relationships have been normal and uneventful. Since those don't make interesting stories, I don't really talk about them. The best stories come from the more unconventional relationships and I have quite a few of those because I like playing there.

My adventures in dating didn't jumpstart my writing about my life, rather it was an encounter I had with a woman I hadn't seen in a few years. We bumped into each other at a party and before I could answer "How are you doing?", she asked "Are you married, yet?" A lot of people ask me that and I always feel I have to have a quip ready: one that seems lighthearted but hopefully also conveys that I think it's a bizarre question. I don't mind being asked if I'm married, but the 'yet' implies that getting married is something I must do. But I never really thought so.

Marriage was never in my plans and I've always thought

that was fine. Not everybody agrees, though. When I'm talking to people-usually women–and they learn I've never been married, some of them look at me with pity. Others look blank, like they're trying to hide their real reaction. Still others look smug, which is particularly funny since many of them don't know where their husbands are half the time, they can barely tolerate being in the same room as their spouse, or they haven't had sex with each other in an eternity. A woman in a genuinely happy marriage is rarely smug. She knows that marriage has its ups-and-downs, that it can be a lot of work, and that she is fortunate that she and her husband have figured it out. The genuinely happily married wife is not smug because she is smarter than that. The smug ones are often working hard to keep a "secret": they're not that happy.

Other women are supportive and encouraging: "Don't worry. He's out there. You just have to keep looking". Sometimes I just smile. When I tell them that I never really wanted a husband, the conversation can get awkward. They may be confused, which is understandable, since most people do want to get married. Some become defensive, though, and those are the ones who amuse me the most. It's as if they think that my decision somehow reflects negatively on them and the choice they made. It doesn't. So I wrote my first essay about my choice not to be a wife or mother. The dating stories came later.

My choosing not to have kids can also slow down a conversation, and gets a similar reaction: most people want children so there's obviously something wrong with the woman who doesn't. But is there?

Here's a story I love. One day, AJ, the son of my friend Lorraine, asked his parents "Is Auntie Eleanore a grown-up?" What I heard was "She's so youthful, she couldn't be as old as you two are!" But what he meant was something different: "…because she doesn't have a husband or any children". Even at four years old, he understood that I hadn't done what I was supposed to do.

Fast forward a few years. The New York Times[1] recently ran an article that talked about the five traditional mile-stones for adulthood: completing school, leaving home, becoming financially independent, marrying, and having a child! What!? This means I'm stuck at stage three. Clearly, AJ isn't the only one who doesn't think I'm a grown-up.

It could be worse. I came across a New York Times article from 1918 called "The Third Sex"[2] that questions whether women who "lack home impulses" (meaning women like me) are real women. So women have come a long way …I think.

Anyway, even though I haven't done what I'm supposed to do (marry, give birth), I'm quite pleased with the way my life has turned out. The growing number of women in the United States who don't have a husband or a child made me decide to share why this doesn't have to be a bad thing. In fact, it can be quite good.

[1] Robin Marantz Henig, "What Is It about Twenty-Something," *New York Times Magazine*, August 22, 2010.
[2] William G. Gregg, "The Third Sex," *New York Times*, September 15, 1918.

A LITTLE BACKGROUND

According to the U.S. Census, 28.3 percent of adults in the United States were unmarried in 1970. That percentage rose to 47.2 in 2010, and a 2011 study by the Pew Research Center found that the number of U.S. adults who are unmarried is now 49 percent, a record low. That's right: almost half of U.S. adults are not married.

To be clear, this number includes not only those who have never married, but also the divorced and widowed. Still, it looks like more and more people are discovering what I already know: being single has a lot of appeal (except, of course, for those who are widowed and didn't really choose their single status).

And if we focus just on the Never Married, that description fits 20.6 percent of white women in the U.S. in 2010, and 41.4 percent of black women.[3]

Interestingly, according to the New York Times, more than half of adults in New York City (where I live) are single. I have no idea what that's about but if you're single and want some like-minded company, New York is the place to be.

Perhaps even more interesting, more women than ever are choosing not to have children. Nineteen percent of women between the ages of 40–44 have no children, which is almost double the percentage from thirty years ago.[4] I find this interesting because it seems there is the belief that if you have a uterus, you should use it, but many are saying "not necessarily."

Anyway, this book is for any grown woman who hasn't married or procreated…maybe for the time being, maybe forever and for the people who look askance at her. Everybody needs to lighten up. Being single without children is not the norm–yet–but there's a lot that's really good about being single, free, and unencumbered. Naturally, there are some trade-offs. This is my story and my own lessons, but I'm hoping that my words will help someone who needs assurance that this can be a really nice life.

[3] U.S. Census Bureau, http://www.census.gov/compendia/statab/2012/tables/12s0056.pdf
[4] U.S. Census Bureau, http://www.nytimes.com/2011/05/10/us/10birth.html

LESSON 1

Marriage. Kids. They're not for everybody.

C'mon guys, there's a reason the divorce rate is as high as it is...and nursing homes are filled with people who aren't being visited by their children. And far, far worse, more than 200 women in the U.S. kill their children each year, according to the American Anthropological Association[5] (but maybe we shouldn't go there.) In any case, it seems silly to expect everyone to follow the same path.

[5] Kelly Banaski Sons, "Why Some Mothers Kill Their Children", December 16, 2005, www.associatedcontent.com/article/14935/why_some_mothers_kill_their_children.html?cat=1.

Recently, Lauren—one of my best friends for 25 years—called me an Old Maid. It began innocently enough. Practicing my Spanish, I had left her a phone message playfully identifying myself as Senorita Wells, and Lauren was kind enough to point out to me that I was too old to be a Senorita. She went on to explain that Senorita (like Mademoiselle and even Miss, to a somewhat lesser extent) refers to a young unmarried woman, not an old unmarried woman. It seemed there was no word for the latter. The concept of a delightful middle-aged woman who has never had a husband (or children) is too far outside of the societal norm to require a designation. So that's when Lauren cheerfully volunteered the Old Maid option. So I stand corrected: there is a term for this poor woman… just not one that I like so much.

So I began a half-hearted search for a word that aptly describes this lifestage of mine. I couldn't be bothered to pick up a dictionary, so I googled "old maid" and the Collins Essential English Dictionary said:

Old Maid, n, A woman regarded as unlikely ever to marry.

Okay, that certainly is me… by my own definition and that of most people who know me. The calls I get from past suitors to ask me out again when they're between relationships of their own often amuse me. I have this vision of them newly single, thumbing through their phone contacts and wondering who they can find to help fill some time. And then my name pops up. When they call, they are usually kind enough to ask if I'm seeing anyone, but I don't think anyone has ever asked if I am now married. They just kind of know.

I kept looking. Answers.com added more color to the old maid definition:

1. Old maid, Offensive. A woman who has remained single beyond the conventional age for marrying.

This definition also fits me, technically, though I don't think I want to adopt it if it's going to offend anyone (although the offense actually applies to me). Plus, I can't help but think of the withered old crone in the Old Maid card deck. When I was growing up, we would play the game whose goal was not to be the player who ended up the Old Maid, which was clearly a bad ending since the Old Maid had scraggly hair, a big nose, and ugly warts. I don't look quite like that so I guess I don't want her representing me. And, fittingly, the deck had only one lonely, pathetic Old Maid card, while all the other cards had a mate because, clearly, that's the way things should be.

At the opposite end of the spectrum is bachelorette, which sounds light-hearted and fun and reminds me of my youth, and cocktails, short dresses, high heels, and unencumbered weekend mornings. That still feels like me, although my gut tells me there's a problem—without me actually having to look it up. *Webster's New World College Dictionary* says:

bach·elor·ette noun
INFORMAL an unmarried, usually young woman.

This definition confirms my suspicions that I passed the bachelorette stage a decade or two ago.

But there's always spinster, which makes me think of Jane Austen. I'm pretty sure this doesn't quite fit me, either, but it's a thought:

Spinster: Archaic : an unmarried woman of gentle family.

While I'm not exactly sure what "gentle family" means, I doubt that it describes mine, though I have a great family. The Encarta Dictionary defines it as "upper class, relating to high social status". I grew up in a blue-collar family in Washington, DC. We're good people, but good solid working class people, so I'd be taking a few liberties with spinster, too, but there's something about it that I like. It's archaic and the idea of resurrecting a word that's past its prime appeals to me. It sounds sturdy and not completely pathetic.

So, spinster it is, at least for now. But why am I not, instead, a wife and/or mother? Lord knows I've been asked that question a gazillion times. My most honest answer, really, is that I must have been absent the day those genes were being given out. I don't have a memory of ever aspiring to be a wife or mother (let's just assume aspiring is the right word). When I played house with Renee, Jackie, and Carla as a kid, everyone wanted to be the mother (who was also a wife), except me. I often agreed to be the man/husband/father, not because I wanted to be a man (I'm straight), but because we were playing make-believe, and I didn't see what the fuss was about. I was happy to accept this role so we could get the game moving along. What difference did it really make? If I remember correctly, I was the only one who felt that way—the only one not vying to play the role of mama.

It's always remarkable to me when I come across a grown woman who brightly declares, "I've known since I was a kid exactly what kind of wedding I wanted." I'm thinking to myself "what is wrong with her?" In all these years, I can honestly say that I've never fantasized about my wedding or what I would name my kids. I don't think I ever actually thought that marriage and kids were necessarily bad, but they never seemed to be for me, and I really was, and remain, puzzled why just about everybody else felt the opposite.

Most of the spinsters I know are kind of spinsters-by-default in that they didn't actively choose it. Some definitely wanted to be married but just weren't able to make it happen. Others were kind of on the fence: wanting it, but not willing to work too hard at it. As far as I know, I'm the only one I know who has gone out of her way to avoid marriage. This used to make me feel kind of weird sometimes–like the proverbial square-peg-in-a-round-hole thing. I often get the raised eyebrow look when I say I actually chose to remain single and childfree. People don't know what to make of it. Now it's their turn to think "what's wrong with her" (meaning me).

I still chuckle, though, at the advice I was given when I was just a spinster-in-training from an older woman who had also managed never to have a husband or child. She told me that I should just "find someone and marry him". Even if I didn't like him very much, I should do it; I only had to stay a little while. Then I could divorce him because, you see "it's better to be a has-been than a never-was!" I'm not sure I buy that, but I know that a lot of people do.

I have been fortunate (fortunate?) enough to have had a few boyfriends who wanted to marry me, so it's not like I didn't get a chance. It just never felt right. And marriage seems really hard. Consistently, whenever I tried to entertain the notion of marriage for even a nanosecond, it was impossible to look 15 years ahead and see that same guy's face. No matter how much I loved him, that image just didn't work for me. How in the world was I supposed to pick someone and stay with him? I don't even plan most of my vacations too far into the future because I might change my mind.

Amelia Earhart - aviator, brave soul, free spirit, and the first person to fly solo over the Atlantic and Pacific Oceans - has come closest to describing my own feelings about marriage. In a letter to her then-fiancé in 1931 she wrote: "I cannot guarantee to endure at all the confinements of even an attractive cage."[6] I get that.

And kids? All I know is that they can be great…for a few minutes. When I'm around them, I spend most of my time pretending like they're cuter and more interesting than I actually think they are. When their parents aren't looking, I pinch them. (Not really).

And here's something I'm finding rather interesting: a rash of studies and articles has appeared lately about how some people are finding that raising kids can be really hard and rather unfulfilling. Maureen Dowd, New York Times columnist, wrote a column about women being increasingly unhappy and cited a study that found that "the one thing in life that will make you less happy is having children".[7] And I think the title of an article in New York Magazine is likewise illuminating: "All Joy and No Fun. Why Parents Hate Parenting".[8] Should this stuff really be a newsflash, though? Kids are cute, wonderful, and delightful, but they're also expensive, time-consuming and a lot of work. Plus, when they grow up, sometimes they lose the cute. (Both articles mention how unwilling people are to admit they wish they hadn't had kids or that their kids were helping destroy their happiness, so I won't belabor this point). Honestly, sometimes I wonder if parents who are concerned that I don't have kids are really members of the misery-loves-company club. Just a thought...

So, here I am: 56 years old, still single, still childfree. While I've (almost) never second-guessed the "no kids" thing, I do sometimes wish there was such a thing as Rent-a-Husband, since a spouse might come in handy at times. When I meet a guy these days, I'm still not seeking marriage, but I am no longer repelled by the thought of something seriously long-lasting. At this age, "till death do us part" isn't that long so it's not so daunting, and I am finally ready to spend some Saturday nights sprawled on the couch rather than on a date. Fortunately, I'm too old to have to even think about kids. Because, really, they're not for everybody.

[6] About.com: http://marriage.about.com/od/historical/a/ameliaearhart_2.htm
[7] Maureen Dowd, "Blue is The New Black", *New York Times*, September 20, 2009
[8] Jennifer Senior, "All Joy and No Fun. Why Parents Hate Parenting," *New YorkMagazine*, July 4, 2010.

LESSON 2

Indulge yourself! Romance. Sex. Adventure.

I like being a woman, and I like being with a man: being courted, flirting, holding hands, laughing over silly double entendres. Something may or may not come of it, and that's okay. I like indulging that part of myself. Having sex is important, too.   It doesn't always have to be LOVE; it's fine that sometimes it's closer to "I think I kinda love you right now".   Under the right conditions, sex is really good for you, good for your body, good for your soul. And God bless Dr. Mehmet Oz who actively promotes sex for its medical benefits (which gives us another reason to do "it"). He says that people who have active sex lives have better cardio health, sleep better and live longer. Honest. He says this a lot. It should be sex-among-equals, though. Meaning: not somebody's husband, and not somebody with whom you really want more, but can't get it. If he's not your significant other, you should both be clear what the deal is. That way, nobody gets hurt and everybody has fun. The adventure part is just pushing the envelope a bit. Dating should be fun... and occasionally doing something out-of-the-ordinary is particularly enjoyable. Dial it up just a little bit. You'll look back at it and smile for years to come. I promise.

I moved from Washington, DC to New York in 1981. I was 26 and just delighted to be here. I initially moved to Hackensack, New Jersey, because I didn't know any better. Nothing against Hackensack; I just belong in New York City. So three months after I moved to New Jersey, I moved to New York, specifically Manhattan. To me, that's where all the action was and I needed to be a part of it. I didn't know many people, so each weekend I'd eagerly set out on my own to discover something new. Looking back, I'm reminded of the line in Stevie Wonder's song, "Living For The City": "Wow. New York City. Skyscrapers and everything!" It was all so exciting. One weekend, I found myself in Greenwich Village. I had only been in New York a few weeks, and this was one of my first stops. I thought the Village was electrifying. I walked around Christopher Street, then turned onto West 4th Street and that's where one of my favorite adventures began.

A guy approached me. He said he'd been watching me from his friend's window and liked what he saw, so he decided to come down. He was low-key and non-threatening, but hearing that I was being watched from a window spooked me a little bit. He introduced himself, giving the name of a well-known, A-list actor. I didn't believe him, of course. He did look a lot like him, though. I became a little confused…then my guard went way up. The monologue in my head was: "This guy can probably tell I'm a bit of a hick from out-of-town, and he thinks I'm gullible. He knows he looks like Mr. Famous Actor and thinks I'm stupid enough to believe that he is". I let him know in no uncertain terms that I wasn't about to be duped. He pulled out his Screen Actors Guild card to prove that he was who he said he was. The card had the name of Mr. Famous Actor. But I still didn't believe him. It's not hard to get a fake i.d.; how hard could it be to get a fake SAG card? By this point, I was getting a little uncomfortable because this guy had put a little too much effort into impersonating this actor, so I went inside a Gristedes grocery store to ask a manager or someone to get this nut away from me. He followed me inside. Then the manager came over and excitedly shook his hand. And the customers in the store smiled and pointed. Oh! I quickly realized that this guy was who he said he was! Wow. Ok. So I gave him my telephone number. He wrote it on a $20 bill because neither of us had any paper. I was excited.

I went home grinning, hardly believing what just happened, and thinking: is this what living in New York is like?! I do belong here! And of all the women in NYC that day, he chose me, which really jazzed me. (It was only later that I learned that this particular actor had a penchant for picking up young, black women and that scores of others had this same story. I didn't care).

He called me that night. For days, I had been begging the building Super to come and fix something, and it had gotten testy between us because I thought he was taking too long and he thought that I was a pain. Anyway, the Super finally decided to show up at my apartment at the moment I was on this very important phone call with Mr. Famous Actor and I wasn't about to get off. I didn't tell him who I was talking to (who would believe me?), and I wouldn't get off the phone to talk to him, either. I know the Super decided at that moment that I was both a pain and a little nuts. The Actor and I made plans to get together the next day. I tried on a dozen outfits trying to find just the right one. I wanted it to look just right: cute and pulled together, but not like I was trying too hard. I didn't want it to be too dressy because that would be corny. I wanted casual, but chic. I decided on a white button-down shirt that would show only a tiny bit of cleavage, linen pants that fit me really well, and my favorite high heels. In retrospect, I don't think I pulled off the right look, though, because I wore purple tights under my pants. I'm not sure I really understood chic back then.

I could barely concentrate at work that day, but I didn't dare tell anyone what I was doing that evening. They might think that the new girl was a kook. I left work and hopped in a cab. I showed up at his apartment which was in a hotel near Columbus Circle. I was a little embarrassed because I was wondering if the lobby manager thought I was a hooker; he looked at me with what I thought was a bit of a smirk. Anyway, he buzzed me up, I got in the elevator, and Mr. Famous Actor opened the door before I could knock. He made a clumsy move that started out like a hug but ended up being more of a pat on my shoulder.

Once inside, I looked around, feeling nervous but hoping that I was looking very cool and calm. His suite was nice but fairly ordinary except it was filled with flowers and a huge chocolate leg, all congratulations for some award or honor he'd just received. We made awkward small talk for a couple of minutes and then he asked what I wanted to do. I had come straight from work and was hungry. Plus, I guess I thought all dates were supposed to start with dinner (this was a date, wasn't it?). We grabbed a bite to eat in the hotel restaurant downstairs and I proceeded to have the most boring date of my entire life! In fact, it was dreadful. I was still a little nervous, and he was practically mute —not exactly the formula for a stimulating evening. What I know now is that this Actor is well-known for not being much of a talker, often giving interviewers shrugs and one-word answers to their questions. But I didn't know that then. I didn't know what was wrong, but I knew what we were doing wasn't working. We finished eating, and I made up an excuse to leave. I couldn't tell if he cared or not. I was so confused. Here I was brand-new to New York City, out with Mr. Famous Actor, which should be the most exciting thing I've done and yet …nothing.

When I got home, I felt a little more clear-headed. I decided I could have handled the situation more cleverly, so I called him, and was pleased that I didn't really have to say much. We made plans to get together the next afternoon. I took the day off. I wanted this time to go better, and I didn't need the distraction of work. So I went there with high hopes and when I arrived, we hugged at the door. Inside, we made more awkward attempts at conversation (this guy was giving me one-word answers), while I was trying to decide where to sit. There weren't a lot of choices. Most of the chairs had piles of stuff, lots of paper and boxes, so the bed would actually be easiest, but that would be too obvious. As I was standing and wondering if he'd clear off a chair for me, he kissed me. It was nice; now we're getting somewhere. And, of course, we continued —all the way, as they used to say. Wow! I don't remember much about the act itself, except giddily thinking, "I can't believe I'm actually doing this with Mr. Famous Actor." It was surreal.

We took a quick nap after and watched some TV…and made much better small talk this time, for some reason that I don't know. Later, while I was showering, I thought, "I can't believe I'm in Mr. Famous Actor's shower…touching all his soap, using his deodorant, drying off with his towels". This was a long way from Nicholson Street, where I grew up. I liked the way he watched me while I got dressed, though he didn't say much, except that he was leaving town later that week for a movie he was shooting. "Okay," I said. "I'll see you when you get back". I didn't, though, unless on the Big Screen counts. That ended my first NYC adventure.

LESSON 3

If your ex was a jackass the first time around, he probably still is.

The success of a revisited relationship depends on why you broke up the first time. It could be a good idea if the reason for the break-up was situational, that is, if there was something going on in your life or his life that got in the way of the relationship (e.g., work, school, distance, immaturity) and that situation has been re-solved. However, if the reason for the break-up was personality-related, don't waste your time. He's just like he was before…only older.

Not too long ago, I reconnected with a guy I had dated 15 years earlier. The first time around was interesting in a peculiar kind of way. If I had wanted a serious relationship, I never would have gone out with him. He was charming, but also known to be a little slippery; however, I didn't want to get married so I could just have fun dating him without having to consider where this could go. This relationship was perfect for that mode of thinking. I liked him, even though I never really penetrated the surface. For the most part, our interactions in the second year were just as superficial as they were in the second month. Neither of us knew how many siblings the other had, each other's birthdays, or lots of other things you'd imagine friends just know about each other. We played totally in the moment. But he was fun, so from time to time over the years after it ended, I wondered if he could have been The One if our relationship had been different, even if I was never really sure what The One meant for me. It was a provocative notion, based on not much at all.

Given that our relationship was spontaneous and not at all deep, there was no real reason to imagine there should have been more, but I think I was just really curious about what was beneath the surface. I wondered if it would have turned out differently - more favorably - if we had done things differently. So I decided to find out what would happen if I agreed to a do over.

I'd always found him intriguing. He wasn't physically attractive. One of my friends thought he looked like a camel, but he was really smart, and funny as hell. He was far from perfect, but I didn't mind at all because (1) so was I, and

(2) how boring would perfect be? I've always preferred to err on the side of rogue.

We weren't serious, so we weren't monogamous. We had what could be called a "don't ask, don't tell" policy that we never even discussed; we just understood. My reason was because, though I liked him a lot, there was always a void there that I looked to others to fill. I imagine he had his reasons.

When we were finally done with each other the first time, it ended quietly. There was no big blowup; I was angry and hurt, but just kinda sucked it up. We didn't even talk about it. He had behaved badly and was cowardly about it. We (okay, I) simply stopped speaking because the situation was just too preposterous to even discuss.

Here's what happened: he had a baby and somehow neglected to mention it to me until she was about six months old. (Actually, he had two, but I'll get to that). Now, because we were both seeing other people, I do understand how this could happen. I'm pretty sure, though, that he was still supposed to mention to me that he impregnated someone and would soon be a father. In fact, he probably should have told me, say, six months before the baby was born, not six months after. So, that ended that. He had a new family to tend to and I wasn't speaking to him, anyway. I was pissed that he hadn't been upfront about this whole scenario.

Within a year or so, he started to reappear. He thought we could pick up where we left off. I wasn't sure this was a good idea but babies do happen sometimes and the parents don't always work it out. I must not have been very busy with anyone important at that moment, and I did have to do some mental gymnastics to make his spinelessness okay. He worked hard at trying to talk me into why we should start seeing each other again. Then, before I could get to "yes", he got the same chick pregnant a second time! Yep. It happened while he was trying to convince me to give him another try, and again he was too chickenshit to tell me. I heard about it from a friend.

After that, I didn't speak to him for years, though I ran into him often. Our circle of friends overlapped a bit, so I couldn't avoid seeing him. At first, my stomach would hurt, but soon I didn't really care. I felt kind of sorry for him. I mean, really, who has two kids "by accident?" Nevertheless, over the years, more than one friend would occasionally urge me to reconsider him. He, too, put in quite an effort at this. He even started getting his hair cut at the barber shop a half block from my apartment, even though we lived nowhere near each other…and he's bald. He did this either to catch a glimpse of me or to aggravate me – possibly a little of both. The very thought of reconciling was mostly laughable to me, though sometimes when I was between relationships I'd remember his charm and ponder "what if."

History books, pop culture, and the wedding section of many newspapers are rife with stories with happy endings from relationships revisited. So, why not give it another shot? We were 15 years older, which I chose to interpret as wiser. We were armed with details of what happened the first time around, so we should be able to do better. Plus, surely he was all the things he was before (still smart, still funny) and was presumably smarter about how to have a relationship with me. I certainly considered myself to be better in every way. With all this in our favor, it should go better this time.

I went from thinking of this reconnection as absurd to actually becoming pretty excited about it. And what a nice story it would make! Most of the women I mentioned it to loved the idea. Interestingly, one male friend Mr. X and I had in common was sure that this was not a good idea: "I don't doubt that he wants to do this; I just don't think he can. He doesn't know how". Well that response wasn't exactly the endorsement I was expecting. This would be a romantic story and our friend obviously didn't understand that. Deep down, I was having my own doubts about whether this was more about the fantasy than the reality, but I pushed those doubts away.

So, we agreed to go for Round Two, 15 years later. This is a one-sided tale so I cannot explain why he made such a big effort to woo me back, only to begin to move in v-e-r-r-y-y slow motion as soon as I said "okay." I suggested we see a movie for our first official date, and then I didn't hear from him for two weeks. That was my first clue that this revisited relationship was not a good idea. Perhaps I wasn't wiser after all given that I ignored this bright red flag and did not step away as quickly as I should have. Short story shorter, the relationship didn't go that well the second time around either, for most of the reasons it didn't go well the first time (minus more babies, as far as I know).

One final Saturday night, he called while I was having dinner with a friend to see if I wanted to get together. He was playful and flirtatious and it sounded like fun, so I wrapped up dinner early, called to say "my place or yours" and was stunned when he then said he couldn't really do it because he was busy preparing for his kids the next day. What? At that moment I decided this was just stupid, and I'd had enough. He was twisted in a way that I couldn't understand, which made it really easy to pull the plug right away; maybe I was a bit wiser.

After the excitement I initially felt at giving what-might-have-been another shot, I thought I'd feel sad when I ended it. Instead, I just felt relieved. This time I understood, really understood, something I believed after our first breakup but chose to talk myself out of once I decided to go back in: the way he handled the situation 15 years ago said he was pretty messed up back then, too.

So what did I learn? Sometimes the second time around isn't so much better, the opposite of what that song by Shalamar says. Sometimes it's even more ridiculous.

LESSON 4

If you don't get married, who's gonna fix that?

Deciding not to get married does involve some trade-offs.

I woke up slowly this particular morning, looking forward to an easy, low-key day. I was visiting my friend, Colleen, in Chicago. We had a fun evening the night before, a great dinner at Nick's Fish Market where the waiters thought we were lesbians on a date, then came home for more cocktails and girl talk. We were up late, stretched out on different corners of the sofa talking way past midnight, with the news of Michael Jackson's mysterious death as background noise on the television. We had planned a lazy day because we'd both had a full work week.

As I was emerging slowly into my morning, the sound of an incoming text message startled me. It was a little too early for a Saturday, which I guess is the reason I looked at it; it might be important…and it was. My tenants had no water. Not a drop. And with two babies in the house, this constituted an emergency.

I bought a house in the Hamptons in 1996 when the walls of my NYC co-op started to close in on me and I decided that—as much as I loved living in the city—I needed another place, a get-away for weekends, vacations, or whenever I wanted a little more space or some quiet.

I love my house. It's a wonderful retreat with enough space to easily entertain friends and family, a backyard where my dog can run around without a leash, and a pool to cool off from the heat or just lay beside and look cute. From time to time when I want to make a little extra cash, I'll rent out the house. This was one of those times.

There had been problems with the well on and off for about

a year, so I had recently begun the process of having new lines laid that would allow me to tap into the town water supply. So I knew the reason the tenants didn't have water was probably complicated–so much for an easy morning.

I immediately got a headache. I hate having to deal with household repairs. Every time I have to have work done on my house, I feel like I have the word sucker stamped on my forehead. I'm always afraid I'm going to be ripped off, and sometimes I am. This makes me dread what has to happen next: I have to call the people working on the well. I have to call the plumber who's laying the water pipes. I decided to also call a real estate agent-friend who lives near my house simply because she knows more than I do about this stuff. I wanted to ask her what I was even supposed to be saying when I called these people because I had no idea. Sigh. I really wasn't up to this. I wished my husband would just take care of it. (Beat) Oh, yeah.

It's times like this that I question my whole "I don't really want to be married" thing. If I was married, I could sweet-ly look at my husband and he would say, "Don't worry, babe. Go back to sleep. I'll take care of it." Wouldn't he? I'm sure he would.

Once I saw a mouse at this same house. I screamed, grabbed the dog, then left and didn't return for almost three months. I'm afraid of mice. I overpaid someone to go in, catch the mouse, catch any of his relatives that might be visiting, and do something to make sure they never came back. If my husband had been there with me, he would have caught and disposed of the mouse, comforted me and let me know everything was going to be alright, and I could have continued to enjoy my house for those three lost months. Plus, I could have bought shoes with the money I paid to de-mouse the place. I needed a husband that night.

And then there was the time a tragedy occurred in the apartment above mine and maggots infested my bathroom as a result. My husband would have taken care of this.

The same principle applies to car maintenance. I love driving around in my convertible Volvo, but every time I took it to the dealership for routine servicing, they would find something wrong that I had no idea was even a problem. I usually didn't believe them, but what could I do? So I paid for work on my car that I may or may not have needed. They wouldn't have treated me like that if I had a husband. But since I didn't, I started taking the car somewhere else, even though it meant breaking the terms of my warranty.

When I was remodeling the bathroom in my apartment, my boyfriend at the time was a big help…kind of like a husband would have been, but also, kind of not. He helped me pick out the right kind of tiles and fixtures, and decided it would be a good idea to rework some of the plumbing since the work involved breaking up the walls anyway. I wouldn't have thought of that. But then he caught an attitude about something and stopped coming around. That's why I bought the wrong toilet–three times. My husband wouldn't have stopped coming around, mostly because he'd be living here, but also because he would want this process to be smooth and easy for me.

Although I'm really good at being single and I like it a lot most of the time, sometimes it doesn't work. Without a doubt, a husband would come in handy a whole host of times. Besides home and car maintenance, the other chores a woman (well, me) shouldn't have to do because hubby would take care of them include:

- Taking the dog for his night shift walk when it's cold or raining
- Pumping the gas
- Killing bugs and throwing out the remains
- Going to get the car so I don't have to walk to the garage in my stilettos
- Escorting me to yet another wedding
- Carrying big things
- Moving heavy stuff
- Changing the light bulb in the bedroom ceiling light fixture because it's too high for me to reach, even standing on a chair (I don't have a ladder)
- Seeing to it that we have a ladder

A boyfriend is not the same as a husband. When I'm seeing someone and these things need to be done, the boyfriend will often do them, but it's not the same because I usually have to ask. I wouldn't have to ask my darling husband. He would just know. Except I don't have one…

LESSON 5

If your husband doesn't like you, he might kill you.

I'm in no danger here. Most women who are murdered are killed by the men they married. My sister spinsters and I are safe. This is not at all funny...though I do find it ironic since your husband is supposed to protect you.

50 Husbands Who [May Have] Killed Their Wives*

1. Scott Peterson murdered pregnant Lacy –exact cause of death unknown–about December 24, 2002.

2. Drew Peterson drowned his third wife Kathleen Savio around March 1, 2004, and he is believed to be responsible for the death of Stacy Peterson, his fourth wife.

3. Henry the VIII beheaded Anne Boleyn on May 19, 1536, and Catherine Howard on February 13, 1542.

4. Charles Stuart fatally shot his pregnant wife, Carol, on October 23, 1989.

5. Robert Blake [is thought by some to have] fatally shot Bonnie Lee Bakley on May 4, 2001.

6. Mark Hacking fatally shot pregnant Lori around July 19, 2004.

7. Neil Entwistle fatally shot Rachel (and infant, Lillian) on January 22, 2006.

8. Shaun Rudy shot and dismembered pregnant Christine on November 12, 2005.

9. Brad Cunningham beat Cheryl to death on September 21, 1986.

10. Quinton Ray strangled Sue Ann in August, 2005.

11. Allen Blackthorne hired Joey Del Toro to fatally shoot Sheila Walsh Bellush on November 7, 1997.

12. Steven Sherer was convicted in June, 2000 of murdering Jami 10 years earlier, around September 30, 1990 (The body was never found).

13. Jeffrey MacDonald fatally stabbed Collette (and

their two daughters) on February 17, 1970.

14. Scott Douglas bludgeoned Ann Scripps Douglas with a hammer on December 31, 1994.

15. Perry March was convicted August 17, 2006 for killing Janet in 1997, (body never found) .

16. Michael White murdered pregnant wife Liana in July 2005. Cause of death was undetermined due to decay.

17. Christian Longo strangled Mary Jane and their three children, in late December 2001.

18. John List fatally shot Helen (and his mother and three children) on November 9, 1971.

19. Fred Neulander paid Len Jenoff and Paul Daniels to bludgeon his wife, Carol on November 1, 1994.

20. George Marecek beat and drowned Viparet , June 3 1991.

21. Mick Fletcher shot his pregnant wife Leann, August 14, 1999.

22. Raymond Wood shot to death Tina (and four of her children) , February 14, 2000.

23. Dickie F. Wimmer fatally shot his wife (and two children) January 15, 1979.

24. Fred Tokars paid Curtis Rower to fatally shoot Sara, November 29, 1992 .

25. Andrew Byrne strangled Leona Caramanica in 1992.

26. Warren Powell strangled Mary Ann, October 1, 1994.

27. Ralf Panitz strangled ex–wife Nancy Campbell in July, 2000.

28. Craig Rabinowitz strangled Stephanie May 6, 1997.

29. Rob Marshall hired a hitman to kill Maria, September 6, 1984.
30. David Brame fatally shot Crystal, April 26, 2003.
31. Eric Bechler drowned Pegye in 1997.
32. Mark Barton beat Leigh Ann (and their two kids) to death with a hammer on July 29, 1999.
33. James Sullivan hired a hitman to fatally shoot Lita in 1987.
34. Dr. Richard Illes fatally shot his estranged wife, Miriam, January. 15, 1999.
35. Richard Sharpe fatally shot Karen in November, 2001.
36. John Sharpe fatally shot pregnant Anna (and infant daughter) with a spear gun in March, 2004.
37. Dr James Klindt killed and dismembered Joyce in March, 1983.
38. Richard Greist fatally stabbed pregnant Janice (and a daughter and the family cat) May 10, 1978.
39. Dr. Yazeed Essa poisoned Rosemarie, February 24, 2005.
40. Dale Huebner strangled Carla on January 6, 2002 with a necktie she had given him for Christmas.
41. Justin Barber fatally shot his wife April in 2002
42. Michael Blagg fatally shot Abby (and daughter) in November 2001.
43. Scott Dunn beat Brandi to death with a hammer on January 14, 2006.
44. Michael Peterson beat Kathleen to death with a fireplace poker on December 9, 2001.
45. Robert A Fratta fatally shot Farah on November 9, 1994.
46. Stephen Grant strangled Tara Lynn on February 9,

2007.

47. Phillip Bond beat his wife Janis to death (and strangled and slashed their two kids) in 2000.

48. Aaron Scott Finney fatally shot Sadie on April 18, 2007.

49. John Hightower fatally shot Dorothy (and her two daughters) on July 12, 1987.

50. And then there's OJ Simpson. He was acquitted, but many believe he slashed Nicole Brown (and Ron Goldman) on June 12, 1994.

*For each case, the husband is widely believed to be guilty, though a few were acquitted or never formally charged.

LESSON **6**

Know who you really are, not who you wish you were.

Even though I didn't want kids, I used to pretend that I would be actively involved with other people's kids. I was slow to realize that the reason I didn't want my own is probably the same reason I'm not all that interested in anybody else's.

Ihave the world's cutest dog. He's an 11-year-old, 10 lb. Yorkie with quite the personality. His name is Danny and for the three years I dated a man with that same name, I spent too much time peppering my conversations with references to Dog-Danny and Man-Danny, just so no one would be confused about which Danny I meant. Dog-Danny can be a bit of a handful. His haircuts cost more than mine and he really is about all the additional responsibility I can handle.

But sometimes I wish I was more like my friend and fellow spinster, Vita. Actually, I don't want to be more like her...I just wish I wanted to. She loves other people's kids. In fact, she more than loves them, she nurtures them, she grooms them, she hangs out with them. She takes them to the movies, out to lunch, out to dinner, has them over for the weekend, lets them spend the week at her house. She's really into them and it seems to bring her a lot of joy. I love my friends' kids, too. I'm always happy to see them and love to hear what they've been up to, but that's pretty much where it ends. I've always known I didn't really want kids of my own, but I used to think I'd be the kind of cool auntie that would have other people's kids over for pajama parties on the weekend, expose them to cultural events, and just sort of hang out with them and talk about things they didn't want to discuss with their parents. It turns out I am not that person.

Yet I am always available to babysit. Said another way, on the rare occasion my friends ask me to babysit, I always say "yes" because it is so very clear that if they're asking me then they're really desperate. If they're asking me to babysit, they have exhausted every other possible avenue. I agree because it's an emergency, so I make myself available.

Babysitting exhausts me because it requires paying attention to the kids. Each time I agree to this, I envision that I'll give them a book and some juice and crackers, and they'll sit happily at the table reading or coloring and enjoying their snack. That has never happened. I always forget that it's not enough to keep them fed, clean, and safe. I actually have to engage with them...which interferes with my newspaper reading or my nap or my phone call or my quiet time.

One Sunday evening, Felicia left 9-year-old Peter with me while she went off to meet some colleagues for dinner. It was nice. I hadn't seen Peter in a few years and we had fun just chatting and catching up on what he'd been doing. We probably spent an hour just doing that. He was growing into a nice young man. We killed more time going out for pizza and walking the dog. And then I realized we were about to have a problem. Sex and the City (SATC) was about to come on. Even though I don't have kids, I read somewhere that a responsible adult does not allow children to watch age-inappropriate shows, especially those with profanity, nudity, and sex. Well, SATC has all those things; that's why I watched it. And that night was going to be no exception. The problem was: what to do with Peter? I would tell someone else in this situation that SATC is not appropriate for a 9-year-old to watch. That rule was about to change. I thought maybe I could use the show as one of those "teachable moments" I'd heard about. Maybe it's okay for a 9-year-old to watch if we discuss the what-not-to-dos on the show. That's how I decided to play it.

After about 10 minutes, though, I could see there wouldn't really be any teachable moments…just a lot of scenes of Samantha hopping into bed with different men.

I felt irresponsible, so I asked Peter to amuse himself in my bedroom with a book until the show was over. I shut the door. An alternative would have been for me to tape the show and watch it later. I didn't think about that as an alternative at the time, though. Next up was The Sopranos, an hour-long show with sex, nudity, profanity, and violence –probably not right for a kid. Yet I knew he wouldn't stay in my bedroom for another hour since he had already asked to come out twice. I decided it was time for Peter to learn about the New Jersey mob. We watched The Sopranos together and I hoped his mother wouldn't be mad at me.

One Saturday, my phone rang about 7 p.m. The babysitting plans of my good friends Derek and Susan had fallen through and they were on their way to a dinner party. Could they drop the kids off at my house for "awhile" ("awhile" turned out to be about five hours). They assured me this would be really easy because the kids would probably be asleep by 9 p.m. Idiot that I am, I believed them. Fortunately, they came armed with videos so I let them watch them for awhile. Kira and Dillon are both really smart and funny, and I had a good time listening to them and laughing at their escapades. They have very active social lives and I get a kick out of hearing about them. Later, I offered them their choice of some kid-appropriate fruit: apple, banana, peach, grapes. Kira decided she wanted my blueberries. The blueberries that cost $5.99/lb. I explained to her that 4-year-olds don't like blueberries but she didn't believe me. She ate them and I made a mental note to hide the expensive fruit the next time she visited. Then, I decided it was time for bed; we piled up in my bed and Dillon asked me to read to them from his favorite book. I was happy to; this was just like on TV. They should fall asleep before I finished the story. At least that's the way it's supposed to work. Instead, when I finished reading, he asked me to read it again. I did. And again. The third time I skipped a few paragraphs because I was sick of this story. Rather, I should say, I tried to skip a few paragraphs because Dillon was on to me. "Uh-uh Auntie Eleanore, that's not how it goes". Why was he still awake anyway?

I thought that if I turned out the light, they would lay quietly and soon fall asleep. They didn't. So I decided to get creative. I decided to tire them out…outside. When I asked them if they wanted to go for a walk, they were surprised but excited because it meant they could get out of bed. By then, it was 10 p.m. There's a lot going on at 10 p.m. on a Saturday night in Chelsea. We wandered around the all-night drugstore, watched oddly dressed people coming in and out of a couple of nightclubs, and saw two men kissing. We walked around for quite awhile just taking in the sights and they fell fast asleep as soon as we got home. When their parents finally showed up to get their kids, they asked how I'd gotten them to sleep. I told them. One found it amusing; the other one didn't.

I never learn. I always have a notion in my head about how these babysitting gigs are going to go and I'm always wrong. I agreed to watch Baldwin and Ford while their parents went off to do God-knows-what. I was looking forward to it because I had never babysat them and I knew I'd enjoy hanging out with them. And it was fun; I was enjoying them…until it was time to feed them. One wanted pizza and the other wanted a burger. I lectured them on how when I was growing up everybody ate the same dinner. They didn't care. I was too tired to argue. They each got the pizza and burger they wanted. I threatened them that next time they'd have to eat the same thing, or starve.

Another time, my darling 8-year-old nephew, Dexter, came to spend a week with me. I was looking forward to this very much. I had never spent a week with a child, and I thought it would be pretty cool for both of us. By day three, though, I was baffled beyond belief. How is it possible for a child to eat all day long? I eat a pretty healthy diet and know that if I had children, they would love their healthy diet, consisting primarily of tasty vegetables and fruit, but not a lot of salt, artificial ingredients, or fried food. The same would be true for any child I'm taking care of. Fast food would only be an occasional treat. Ha! I quickly learned it's not possible to cook enough food to feed a growing boy. He was like a bottomless pit. I happily decided that I was wrong about fast food and that it is not a bad thing. In fact, it's a good thing. Otherwise, the poor kid would have starved.

Here's what I know for sure: watching other people's kids is way too much work. I love them a lot, but I don't have it in me. I'm definitely not the cool aunt I thought I'd be. Not too long ago, I pretended to be catching the flu so I wouldn't have to babysit a friend's cute little kid who talks way too much. I really don't know how Vita does it. Or why I thought I could. I, now, really know who I am.

LESSON 7

Laugh at the inanity of it all.

You cannot get annoyed every time someone makes a dumb comment about your unmarried or childfree state. The reality, though, is that the onus is on you to make everybody comfortable. That's just the way it is, and laughter is a great way to do it.

Did you hear the one about…

A decorated war veteran, fresh off the bus, is looking for a place to stay. He hears that room and board is available from the three old spinsters at the edge of town, but is advised they are very picky about letting strangers stay there. He decides to chance it, and limps on up to the front door. Gladys answers his knock.
"What do you want, sonny?" she asks him.

"Ma'am, I'm just looking for a hot meal and a room for the night," he answers.

The other two old spinsters gather around the door. "Who's out there? Does he look decent?" they ask.

Gladys says, "It's a soldier, and he's got a Purple Heart on."

The other two spinsters giggle and say, "The hell with what color it is… let him in!"

❧❦❧

An old spinster was asked what she likes most in men. "Appearance", she replied, "and the sooner, the better!"

❧❦❧

There were two old maid sisters, both virgins. It's Friday night and Gladys looks at Betty and says, "I'm not going to die a virgin. I'm going out and I'm not coming home until I've been laid!"

Betty says, "Well, make sure you`re home by 10 so I don`t worry about you." 10 o`clock rolls around, and there`s no sign of Gladys... 11 o`clock...12 o`clock... Finally about 1:15 a.m. the front door flies open. In runs Gladys, straight to the bathroom.

Betty goes and knocks on the door, "Are you okay, Gladys?" There's no answer, so she opens the door and there sits Gladys with her panties around her ankles, legs spread, and her head stuck between her legs looking at herself.

"What is it, Gladys??? What`s wrong?" asks Betty.

"Betty, it was 10 inches long when it went in ... and 5 inches when it came out. When I find the other half you`re gonna have the time of your life!

An old maid was held up in a dark alley. She explained that she had no money, but the robber insisted that it must be in her bra and started feeling around.
"I told you I haven't got any money." the old maid said.

"But if you keep doing that, I'll write you a check."

Two old maids were grocery shopping. The sign said "Bananas -- 3 for 50 cents." So they put two in the shopping cart.
One said to the other, "How much will that be apiece?"

The other one said, "That would be fifty cents divided by three, multiplied by two, then divided by two–whatever that comes to."

So the first old maid said, "Heck, just get three. That'll be a quarter apiece and we can eat the other one.

∾⊙〜

A small dog and a Great Dane are at the vet and the small dog is very upset. The Great Dane asks, "What's wrong there, buddy?"

The small dog answers, "This is the worst day of my life. My owner is an old maid. Last night she had a date. She had her church choir leader and his elderly mother come over for dinner. When I saw the old woman I don't know what came over me but I ran up to her and started humping her leg. I just couldn't help myself. They pulled me off of her, locked me in the closet, and now I'm here to be neutered."

So the Great Dane says, "I know how you feel there buddy. My owner is an old maid, too. Last night I was walking by the bathroom and she'd just gotten out of the shower. She was bent over drying herself with her back to me when, I don't know what came over me, but I ran up to her, mounted her from behind and started humping her. She started screaming, but I just held on real tight and kept at it until we both passed out on the floor from exhaustion."

The small dog says: "Oh no, so they're going to neuter you too?"

The Great Dane says: "Oh God no! I'm just here to get my nails clipped."

∾⊙〜

What did one old maid say to the other old maid? Let's go down to the cucumber patch and do push-ups!

Jill, a love-starved spinster, was so desperate that she went to a local newspaper office and inquired about putting an advertisement in the Lonely Hearts column.

"Well, madam," the assistant said, "we charge a minimum of $1 per insertion."

You don't say," said Jill. "Well then, here's $20 and to hell with the advertisement! "

On her 70th birthday, a spinster decides it's time to finally get married. Since she has no prospects on the horizon, she decides to run an advertisement in the local newspaper: "Seventy-year-young-at-heart virgin seeks husband. Must be in same age group, must not beat me, must not walk all over me, and MUST still be good in bed. Apply in person." The next day, her doorbell rings, and when she opens the door, much to her dismay is a gray haired man in a wheel-chair, and he has no arms or legs.

She asks the man, "Do you really expect me to pick you? You don't even have any arms or legs!"

The old man replies, "Well, I don't have arms, so how could I beat you?" The woman agrees, and asks him to proceed. "I don't have any legs, so how could I walk all over you?"

Again, she agrees, and replies, "But how could you, without any arms or legs, possibly be good in bed?"

The man smiles and says, "I rang the doorbell, didn't I!"

Keep smiling.

LESSON 8

Be nice to old people.

That could be you one day. Small gestures can make a huge difference in someone's life. Plus, it might be the one action that saves you from going to hell.

When I was a kid, my neighborhood always had an old lady or two who lived alone. My mother would often visit to keep them company, take them food sometimes, occasionally run errands for them or help out with the housekeeping–basically making sure everything was okay. Sometimes she would take me with her and I always thought their houses smelled funny. I would wonder where their families were, but each one had a different story. My mother always seemed to enjoy them. I never really gave much thought to this whole dynamic; it was just the thing to do. You looked out for old people.

Years ago, I read an article in Ms. Magazine (I think) where Gloria Steinem said she had a fear of being homeless one day. Never mind that she was pretty well-off and that this fear seemed somewhat far-fetched. Your fears are your fears, and they don't have to make sense. Mine is that I'll end up in the autumn of my life old and alone, no friends or family or anybody to come around for a visit...at least anybody that I like.

Fast-forward to the present. An old lady lives down the hall from me whose situation scares me a lot. She's in her 80s, in good enough health, and pretty self-sufficient. She never had kids and her husband died decades ago. She lives alone, and I'm pretty sure she's really lonely. I used to think she must have a really horrible family because she speaks of them often, mostly complaining that they don't visit and rarely call. I remember thinking that this shouldn't be, and reminded me of the way my mother looked out for the old ladies in our neighborhood. I began a relationship with her, in part because I don't think anyone should have the good fortune to live this long in good health and yet be unhappy. In the back of my mind I am also terrified that her deal could be mine some day: very old and very alone.

We started a friendship. She and I would visit from time to time; sometimes I'd take her out for a bite to eat or to see a play. She would bring me goodies she'd cooked, and I bought her gifts of things she'd expressed interest in. But as I spent more and more time with her, it became clear to me why–at least to some extent–she was so alone. She's hard to be around: unnecessarily aggressive, difficult to please, and full of complaints about all kinds of things most people don't even notice. At a restaurant, she'd complain that the bread wasn't warm enough, the waiter not well-trained, and the food not prepared properly. At a musical, the orchestra "sounded stiff." Once when another neighbor joined us for brunch, she repeatedly told the newcomer that she "looked ridiculous" because she carried an umbrella on a sunny day. Although she's lived in the U.S. all her life, the Old Lady frequently complains about the ways of life here, as opposed to Greece where she was born, which I'm sure she barely remembers because her family moved here when she was four.

Her company became so trying and unpleasant that I eventually distanced myself from her. I didn't relish telling an 85-year-old woman that her company gave me a stomachache. I began to think her family might not actually be bad people, but just kind of fed up. Still, I felt bad about pulling away, so from time to time (probably not often enough), I still try to find ways to engage her...briefly. When I'm old and alone I hope someone will at least try with me.

A couple of years ago, I became friendly with some kids down the hall. They are a cute married couple who are 20 years my junior (which is what makes them kids). We had had a nodding acquaintance for some time, which evolved to small talk, which eventually grew into real conversation. Our dogs even became best friends. Somewhere along the way our age difference came up. Shortly after that, Traci knocked on my door and brought me dinner one night. I was simultaneously delighted and horrified: delighted because free, good food is one of my favorite things in the whole world, yet horrified because I realized that she saw me as "the old lady down the hall." No matter your age, anybody 20 years older than you is old. So here I am thinking we're peers, and they're thinking "let's take that poor old lady some dinner." Traci is a good and generous cook, so even while I was trying to figure out how offended I should be, I continued to accept her generosity. Part of me wanted to complain about being relegated to such a status, but I was afraid I'd sound like you-know-who. Plus, the food was good and it was free. And it sometimes came with wine. So I said nothing…for awhile.

And then one day I mentioned it to my friend, Lauren, who's not the most cynical person I know, but she comes close. After she finished laughing for a little too long, she gasped that they were adopting me the way all good people adopt the old and infirm. This confirmed that I wasn't imagining it. I finally mentioned to Traci and Tony that I really appreciated their good-heartedness, but that I might be a tad young (right now) for their foster grandparent program. They were kind enough to insist that they were doing this because they actually like me and not because I'm old and alone and look like I could use some help. I am choosing to believe them and so now I take advantage of their kindness on a regular basis. I hope they don't move. All old people need nice young people to look in on them now and then. I'm very lucky to have them. Think "karma". (I wonder if they have any more wine?)

LESSON 9

Use birth control, dammit.

There's no such thing as being overprepared. Honest. If you're not actively trying to get pregnant, do something about it. Otherwise, your new nickname could be Mom.

Ido not know why motherhood was never a serious part of my plan. I assumed that one day I might change my mind…but I never really did. Sex, yes. Baby, no. I was fortunate enough to have grown up at a time when government programs didn't have the bad taint they have now. If you needed, or merely wanted, something in the way of social services, you could probably get it. So that's why I went to a neighborhood clinic near my high school one day. It had a program that would give birth control pills to whoever wanted them. For free. All you had to do was ask (and register). Now, I'm recalling this some 35 years later so the details on the program are fuzzy. I'm sure there were more parameters than I recall, but I do know that at 16 or 17 years of age, I found myself in possession of pills that would help me not get pregnant. Never mind that I was still a virgin. I knew I was getting close to changing my status in that regard and I wanted to be prepared.

And that's pretty much the way I've always approached birth control; very diligently, with not even the chance of a slip-up. When I was between relationships, I'd continue to take the Pill even though I wasn't doing anything that made this necessary. Some of my friends would stop when they weren't dating and would start again when they thought a new relationship was getting to that place where they'd soon be rolling around naked with someone. The problem is that you can't always predict exactly when that will be. Relationships can progress quickly, and a few of my girlfriends got pregnant. Not me. As long as I continued to take my Pills, I was safe. So imagine how furious I was when at the age of 28 I found myself pregnant. I was really mad and felt really stupid. How could I have been so careless?

Here's how. I'd been dating this guy --let's just call him Fred (because I don't think I've ever dated a Fred). We dated for a couple of years. We would go out dancing, take drives to the beach, and order in a fried fish dinner every Friday night from the diner up the street from my apartment. It was a fun, no-drama relationship, as I recall, though I must be forgetting some of the details because we did break up once. I don't remember why. And then he called and wanted to come by. Our plan was to talk about whatever caused the break-up and probably about reconciling. That's it.

 During the time we dated, I had moved off the Pill and was now using a cervical cap (similar to a diaphragm, but smaller and tighter). I had heard somewhere that women should take a break from the Pill from time to time, so I did. I decided on the cervical cap because it was supposedly more effective than the diaphragm and could be inserted up to 24 hours before intercourse. Organized soul that I am, I would always insert the cap the moment I knew I was going to see Fred. This saved me from having to remember to do it later and saved us from having to interrupt the moment. Now, however, we were no longer a couple, and he was just coming by to talk. So that day I left my trusted cervical cap in its case in the drawer by my bed. I wouldn't need it that night because surely he didn't think we were going to "do it" on the first day back!

Except…we did.   We were on the couch in my living room, Lionel Richie was on in the background, and I still remember that "You Are" was playing at that fateful moment at the end, which is precisely when I remembered that I had forgotten something very important. Jumping up didn't help, I later discovered. It's an understatement to call this a seriously big oops.

I'm always amused at the occasional news story about a woman who would give birth and claim she never knew she was pregnant. I knew in about three weeks. I knew even before I missed my period. My nipples were already tender and I just felt funny. Something definitely wasn't right. I was too embarrassed to go to my doctor, so I went to a clinic for a pregnancy test . This was in the days long before you could go to the drugstore and buy a kit that would give you that information in a matter of minutes. I went by myself. The clinic sent me home because it was too soon, and the test was inconclusive. They asked me to come back in a few weeks. Honestly, I didn't need to go back; I didn't really need a test because I knew what my body was telling me: I was pregnant... pregnant with what could become Fred's child. While Fred was a perfectly nice man who I enjoyed a lot, I had no desire to have a future with him. And having a kid with someone –married to him or not–means he's in your future.

I think I waited another two weeks and went back for re-testing. I'll never forget the way the clinic assistant told me what I already knew. She said, "I have bad news." It was indeed bad news, but how did she know I wouldn't be delighted? That was quite an assumption she was making, so I asked. She said with a smile: "I just know; you've got that Jordache look." (Jordache was a popular brand of jeans for young, hip women in the 1980s). Was it that obvious? She was right though. Later, I couldn't get over how embarrassed and stupid I felt. What was I doing accidentally pregnant? I knew better. Yet there I was.

I don't even remember Fred's reaction when I told him because all I could focus on was myself. I do remember that that day was the first time I'd heard Michael Jackson's new song, Billie Jean, about a suspect pregnancy. It didn't directly relate to my situation, but it still felt a little ironic to be hearing this song right around the same time I was telling Fred that I was pregnant. I think I had already scheduled the abortion when I told him; he didn't object, but it wouldn't have mattered if he had. I just thank God for Planned Parenthood and organizations like that because I knew I could go there and have a safe procedure in a clean and supportive environment, and that I would be well taken care of. Fred met me there, looking terrified, probably scared that I would change my mind. No chance of that. The doctor and staff were nice, caring, and efficient. I felt very calm. I don't remember much else about that day except the two of us stopping at a KFC for takeout chicken before heading back to my apartment, and me then sleeping for the rest of the day. Fred and I dated for another two years after that and, oddly, only mentioned our almost-parenthood once.

It doesn't really even matter why I didn't want to have a baby. I think if a woman doesn't want a kid, she shouldn't have one. It's too important a decision to be forced into. I know there are many women who have contemplated abortion and are really happy that they didn't go through with it. I don't think I would have been one of those women. I was young and single, didn't have much money, and was still trying to find my way in New York City. I was living the Jordache life. Had I been forced to have the baby, I hope I would have loved it. I'm pretty sure I would have resented it, too, and that's not good for anybody. I've never regretted that decision. And have always been prepared with birth control ever since.

LESSON 10

Try not to be shallow.

I would really like to say here that I've learned to always look past the outer surface and focus on the person within. Let's just say I'm still working on this one.

As a single woman in these modern times, of course I've done online dating. Lots of it. I'm really good at it and have had lots of fun as a result. It's an opportunity to meet the widest range of men imaginable, go out with men I might not ever have met, try out some I might never have considered in ordinary circumstances, and a way to make sure I could have a date whenever I wanted. I once went out with 15 men in one month–a date every other day–just to see what it was like. Actually it was kind of stupid. There are not 15 men in that short period of time that I'm really that interested in…but it did make for great stories. Although not part of that particular experiment, here's an online dating story that really stuck with me.

Nowadays, most people who are doing online dating post a picture of themselves. All the matchmaking sites tell you that you get 10 times more "hits" if you post a picture. But in the early days, we didn't do that. We more or less described ourselves in our profiles and took it from there. Internet dating was too new and it felt kind of creepy to post a picture for the whole world to see. One evening, I was contacted by what seemed like a very nice man. We chatted online for a couple of weeks, eventually talking just about every day; there was some real interest there and it seemed like there might be some potential for something interesting to happen. I wasn't sure if he was my type because he was a little quiet, but he liked a lot of things about New York that I liked, and he said he was really interested in finding the right girl. Maybe I was that girl.

We made plans to finally meet one Friday evening on the

hottest day of the year. We decided to meet for dinner at a restaurant in my neighborhood. (As I became more astute at Internet dating, I learned that you never plan dinner with a stranger. Drinks or coffee–something quick. If you like each other, you can plan on dinner the next time. If you don't, you haven't wasted much time).

As we talked about how we would recognize each other, we realized that we were both wearing fairly nondescript outfits: jeans and a white T-shirt. Rather than change clothes, we tried to think of what we could do to make ourselves recognizable to a stranger in a crowded restaurant. He suggested I put a flower in my hair. My hair was really short so that wouldn't work. I had the brilliant idea to tie a bright pink sweater around my neck. It was a pretty sweater but I felt a little foolish in 100 degree heat with a sweater. Whatever; he needed to be able to identify me. When I got to the restaurant, I couldn't really pick him out of the crowd because half the men in the place were wearing jeans and a T-shirt. He recognized me, though, by my sweater and approached me. In an instant, I started to feel like a real ass and wondered if I was really shallow. I'm afraid I was. He was an albino; it was a deal-breaker.

But I was also confused: should I have expected him to mention that to me at some point during our weeks of conversation? Should it have mattered? I still don't know the right answer. I don't know whether his being an albino should have mattered, but I do know that it did. I was annoyed at myself for feeling this way and I was annoyed at him for leaving out this detail. Plus, why was I walking around in the scorching heat with a sweater? During the "how will we recognize each other" phase of our conversation, he could have easily said "I'll be the albino at the bar." It would have been too rude to leave, though I certainly wanted to. We managed to have a pleasant enough dinner, but I practically inhaled mine and wasn't interested in after-dinner coffee or another drink. I wanted to go home. I couldn't make myself interested in him, no matter how nice he was. We didn't go out again.

Then, this story started to take on a life of its own. The first few people I told this story to agreed they would probably have reacted the same way I did. I felt like a real heel, though, after talking to my friend, Pat. She thought I was disgustingly small-minded and that my behavior was just plain wrong. How dare I think he should have told me ahead of time, and how dare I have the audacity to lose interest over something like this in a man I originally found (somewhat) interesting. The first part of the statement was the most intriguing. How much information–and what kind—do you owe your blind date? Should he have been expected to tell me of his albinism? What if he had a wooden leg? What are the parameters?

I quickly learned that this is a great question to pose at a dinner party because it always generates lively discussion with a range of responses. Albinism is not a disease; it doesn't affect a person's health or personality. It doesn't impact anything, in fact, except a person's melanin level, so makes one look kind of funny. But is that a valid reason for not going out with someone? How should the albino treat it? Like it's a fact of life and of no real consequence? Or should he "warn" the person he's meeting? Oh, don't give me that look; what would you have done? Probably the grown-up lesson here is to look beyond the surface.

LESSON 11

Be patient with women who've lost the ability to talk about anything but their kids.

(Sigh). I really don't know what to do about this issue. Anything I or any other childfree woman says—and no matter how sweetly—will not be received well.

I am fortunate to have a great social circle made up of women who are married and single, with and without children. What follows is a rehash of a conversation I've had many, many times with some of my friends without children (FWOC) about some of our friends with children. We have a complaint, but I first need to make it clear that this does not apply to all our friends with children… just the guilty ones.

Here it is: we would like you to please stop dominating the conversation with stories about your kids. This is a delicate request, and it would be easy to misinterpret, and quite easy to cause hurt feelings. In fact, that's why my FWOC and I only complain about this in private to each other. We wish we could say it to the offending parties but we know we can't. It'll sound mean. Or bitchy. There would be hurt feelings.

You will think we're just jealous that we don't have kids. Worst of all, you'll think we don't love your kids or don't want to hear about them. Neither is true. We do love your kids, and we do want to hear about them…Just. Not. All. The. Time. When The Girls are spending time together catching up and doing whatever it is we do, it's because we enjoy each other's company and want to hear what's going on with each other, which includes you.

Here's what happens too often. We ask how you are, and you tell us how your kids are. We ask what you've been up to, and you tell us what your kids are doing. We ask about good movies you've seen lately, and you tell us about your kids' new favorite movie. We talk about the joys of the Obama election, and you tell us how excited your kids are...saying little about your own thoughts.

Of course, not all women with children are guilty of this.

Here's why this bugs us: It changes the tone and feel of the conversation, and it can't really go anywhere from there. Plus, we actually want to hear about YOU. It's okay to pepper your stories with anecdotes about your kids–we do love hearing about them--- but, really...enough. There's a limit. We want to talk about grown-ups and grown-up things.

My FWOC and I often wonder about this. You've always been interesting, dynamic, opinionated, and fully capable of holding your own in a conversation. That's why we're friends with you. Then something happened. It didn't happen to everybody. But somewhere along the way, the answer to "what have you been up to" became "Johnny just made honor roll for the third year in a row." That's really nice, but here's the issue: it doesn't answer the question. We're with you because we enjoy you, want to hear what you're doing, why you're doing it...and the "Johnny" response doesn't tell us any of that. Then another mother at the table will offer how much Janie is enjoying glee club. So, now we're talking about the kids, not the grown-ups, which means that the women without kids–and the women who don't want to talk about their kids–are left out of the conversation, as it goes from one child-based comment to the next. This could be amusing if our eyes weren't glazing over.

We know that your kids are the most important thing in

the world to you. We agree with you that they're delightful and smart and funny and interesting and wonderful in every way. We like to hear about how and what they're doing–in context. On a few occasions, my FWOC and I have promised each other to change the subject every time the conversation dissolves into kid chatter, and as hard as we've tried, this tactic doesn't work. We now know that there is almost no topic where "my kid" can't be inserted. We've tried going silent, thinking you'd notice that we're not participating in the conversation. You didn't. We've also tried opening the conversation by asking about the kids, believing it should accomplish two things: it would let us know how the kids are doing (because we do want to know), and it would pave the way for a more adult-centered gabfest because we've already talked about the kids. That doesn't work either. (Of course, I'm not talking about all our friends with kids. It is interesting, though, that men don't do this).

What's funny about this is that we're not even looking for highly stimulating conversations. We just want grown-up girl talk. As you know, we, ourselves, are not saying anything deep or thought-provoking...and we want the opportunity to have conversations with you that are as banal as those we're having with everyone else! And honestly, your kids are interesting, but they're not that interesting.

By the way, if you're reading this and ask me if I'm talking about you, I'm going to say "No"...though I might be.

LESSON 12

Pregnancy has its benefits…

…beside the obvious one. You'll miss out on them, though. By deciding not to have kids, we spinsters miss out on these benefits.

Being pregnant has got to be really amazing. Though I've never wanted to have (and especially raise) a child, I wouldn't have minded the experience of a full-term pregnancy...minus the birthing and lifetime commitment. I'm missing out on all kinds of perks. Here are some examples:

- I was with a pregnant co-worker one day and watched her happily eat her way through a bag of jelly beans and a pack of cookies...something she never would have done pre-pregnancy, when she was really careful about what she ate. I don't really want to eat a bag of jelly beans and a pack of cookies, but there's a lot of other stuff I want to eat without having to worry "how will this look around my middle?" If I were pregnant, my diet would consist of unlimited amounts of french fries and gummy bears. Oh, I'd still eat lots of vegetables and other good-for-me stuff, but I would also chow down on boundless quantities of all the goodies I now only eat in moderation. I'd no longer have to worry about getting thick around the middle because getting thick around the middle is exactly what I'm supposed to do. This would make me very happy.

- Once, we let another pregnant co-worker miss a meeting so she could take a nap. I want to miss a meeting so I can take a nap, however it would be frowned upon...unless I were pregnant. I'm a big fan of naps, and now that I'm self-employed, I try to take a nap every day. It's marvelous. My friend, Derek, likes to call me around 3 p.m. or 4 p.m.–the time I prefer to nap–and each time wonders why I'm asleep in the middle of the day when I could be doing something more productive. People who don't understand the glories of napping ask "Are you depressed? Do you feel okay? Is anything wrong?" "Other than you disturbing my nap, no". I try to educate them that many admirable people were proponents of napping. People like Albert Einstein and Winston Churchill and Franklin D. Roosevelt. This puts me in fine company, but people are still judgmental. I don't know what's wrong with them, but I'm tired of it. If I were pregnant, people would understand my naps, and even be sympathetic.

• A pregnant woman is a person-of-interest, in a good way. Everybody you know–and some that you don't–smiles when they see you, and expresses interest in your status like never before: how are you feeling, how many months are you, when's your delivery date, boy or girl, is this your first? Suddenly, lots of people are interested in you...even if you're not that interesting.

• Pregnancy gives some women particularly lustrous hair. It grows long, shiny, and vibrant in a way it never had before. I wouldn't mind that. In fact, I'd like it a lot. All my life I've struggled to get my hair to cooperate. It grows slowly, is much too dry, and is not thick like a horse's mane. My hair just will not do the shiny thing...but maybe it would if I was pregnant.

- A pregnant woman has powerful—and erratic—emotions because her hormones are doing all kinds of wild things. She can cry and rage instantly for things the rest of us don't understand, but we try to be understanding because she's pregnant. I once came across a cartoon of a pregnant woman and her husband talking. The woman in the cartoon says, tearfully, "I hope in your next life you come back as a pregnant woman." He responds "And I hope you come back as the husband of a pregnant woman." I sent this to my friend, Benilde, who was pregnant at the time. Actually, I sent it to her husband. I can't even imagine how wonderful it would be to be able to indulge myself in whatever unreasonableness I wanted…with no real consequences because "I'm pregnant, what do you expect?"

What I need to do is figure out a way to experience all the benefits of being pregnant, without actually having to be pregnant. It would be kind of like having one of those non-drivers licenses for people who don't drive. All the benefits without the hard part.

LESSON 13

Let labels roll off your back.

People want to know why you're a spinster. If you don't give them a good reason (or even if you do), they'll come up with a reason of their own: She's an odd-ball… difficult…angry…too picky. Maybe she's gay. You don't really owe anyone an explanation, though.

At some point, I'm not exactly sure when, I found myself explaining to people that, "no, I'm not gay, I just don't want to get married." Some of them don't believe me. What's funny about that is it's hard to deny that you're not something that people have already decided that you are. If I was gay and in the closet, then of course I would deny it if asked, so denying it doesn't really matter:

- I went to visit a friend in Tulsa one summer. She and I had been friends for many years. In fact, I fixed her up with her husband. We know each other well. She and I were enjoying a leisurely cup of coffee one afternoon while her husband and new baby were out. We were just shooting the breeze, or so I thought. At one point, she took my hand and said "I just want you to know that it's okay if you're gay. I love you anyway." I laughed and said "well, that's really good to know, but what makes you think I'm gay?" "Well, you're still not married…and you wear your hair short…and look what you're wearing; it's kind of unisex. But, really, it's okay." (I'd never thought of it that way; I was wearing one of my favorite outfits: jeans, a white T-shirt, and cowboy boots. It didn't occur to me that it was an androgynous outfit). I told her that despite those observations, I still wasn't gay. We went back and forth about this a few more times. I started to get annoyed because she wouldn't let it go. I also realized that if I got angry she'd swear it was because I'd been found out. So I decided to try really hard to remain calm. Then it occurred to me that if I didn't show enough emotion, she would think it was because it was true and perhaps I was relieved that my secret was out. How funny. We fell into an awkward silence. She said she felt bad that she'd broached the subject before I was ready to talk about it. Geez.

- My co-worker, Mike, admitted to me after we became friendly that he and another colleague had been sure I was gay. Otherwise, why wasn't I married. ("Really?" I'm thinking). When I asked why they thought that, he said it was because not only wasn't I married, but I wasn't close to it, and I didn't complain about it…plus I had a copy of Out magazine on my desk. (Out targets a gay audience). I worked at an advertising agency, and we received most magazines that were published. On my desk along with Out were lots of others including GQ, Sports Illustrated and Seventeen. I'm also not a man nor a teenager, but for some reason having those magazines didn't affect his logic. I found this quite curious; all it took to determine my sexual orientation was a magazine on my desk. I asked if they thought another woman we worked with, Penny (not her real name), was also gay. She, too, was unmarried, had no kids, and was about the same age as I was. They didn't think she was gay because it was clear why she was single: she wasn't that attractive and she was unpleasant. Who would want her? Aha. Somewhere in there was a really backhanded compliment to me…I think.

- My family originates from South Carolina where at one time marriage was the immediate goal for women right after high school graduation. Guys might get a pass for a few more years. At a family reunion, one of my cousins made a couple of sly comments about lesbians and looked to me for a reaction. I didn't really have one at first, until I realized I was being baited. My conversation with my Tulsa friend flashed through my head: any reaction that's too strong or not strong enough would determine that I must be guilty. I decided to try laughing it off. That didn't seem to help much, either. As the day went on and the conversations became looser, she pointed out that the ring I was wearing on my thumb was a way to let other lesbians know I was part of the tribe. (How did she know that? I didn't). By now, I'd learned that it didn't really matter what I said, so I didn't say much. Of course, that only served to reinforce the thought. So now the whole family "knew." (Sigh).

- Once my friend, Lori (a fellow spinster), came to visit me at my vacation home in Long Island. It was a beautiful Saturday afternoon in the fall and we thought it would be fun to go apple picking. We were really looking forward to it as we drove out to the farm because nothing tastes better than a just-picked apple. We would use some of the apples for pies, maybe bake a few with a little butter and brown sugar, or just enjoy them plain. Once we got to the farm, we had to take a hayride to the orchards. This was going to be even more fun than we had anticipated. After we boarded, though, we realized that only two kinds of people take Saturday evening hayrides: (1) families with children, and (2) couples (it was kind of romantic). Lori and I were neither...except we apparently were a couple, as far as most everyone else was concerned. We were two middle-aged ladies on a date. We got quite a few longer-than-necessary glances. And the hayride driver, bless his heart, made it a point to make us feel welcome and included.

After a number of such experiences, I eventually became self-conscious, which was stupid. I wasn't gay (not that there's anything wrong with it, for you Seinfeld fans), and I didn't want people to think I was. I also happen to live in Chelsea, a NYC neighborhood with a higher-than-average gay population, which didn't really help. It really shouldn't have mattered, but I guess it did.

My friends Lauren and Benilde (both married) like to hold my hand as we stroll Manhattan doing girly things. I put a stop to it. "Don't touch me; people already think I'm gay. They'll see me holding hands with you and it's confirmed!" They told me I was stupid. I agreed..."but let go of my hand anyway." I finally realized that the concept of a woman not wanting to be married makes no sense to a lot of people. She should at least want it, even if it doesn't happen. What I need to do is complain more, and pretend that I'm dying to be married if only I could find someone who would have me. That would make much more sense to people. Then I would be normal.

LESSON 14

You're not losing a girlfriend, you're gaining a *boy*friend.

Sometimes women complain that friendships end when their friend gets married. That's probably true if the friendship is mostly rooted in activities that the "bride" no longer engages in. If she's not going to the club anymore or has less time to hang out, then the friendship probably will end, or at least change. However, if there's a real emotional connection, the friendship will be fine. If you genuinely like each other, marriage won't change that. She's still your girl. Relax. Plus, if you like her husband, you just gained a new friend.

My sisterhood of spinsters (not that we ever called ourselves that), has changed. Some of my spinsters-in-crime, have left the fold. Cindy, Lorraine, Nancy, and Pat are dear friends who were single way past the national average. I miss hanging out with them. Oh, we still hang out, but not in that "maybe there'll be some cute boys there" kind of way. I could always count on Lorraine for a party. Cindy and I had lots of dinners around town at trendy NYC restaurants, and Nancy even tricked me once into going away for the weekend to the Newport Folk Festival (I thought she said Jazz Festival). I could always count on Pat to be ready within minutes for a drink…or whatever else we thought up. Now they're all married. Each one married late in life, and each married well. They were over 40 and though some would have preferred to have done the deed earlier, I think they're all pretty pleased with where they landed. I'm certainly pleased for them. Their stories actually help me view marriage more positively, as I think each one got the man she was supposed to have.

Many years ago, a study claimed that the odds of a woman over 40 getting married were the same as the odds of her getting attacked (or was it kidnapped?) by terrorists. (On September 11, 2001, my sister Phyllis --with her own special style of humor-- informed me that I could now marry, given that the terrorist attack had occurred…but that's another story).

The gist of the study actually turned out to have been widely misreported. I don't recall what the actual findings were, but the version that was repeated most often was certainly more interesting than the truth. At any rate, first-time marriage for women over 40 is more common than it used to be. Apparently, single women over 40 now have a 41% chance of marrying, vs just 1% a few decades ago.[9] What I like about this is that, speaking from my own personal experience, the folks I know who've gotten married later in life seem to have chosen very well. Their marriages truly seem to be the "till death do us part" type, whereas many weddings for those who are younger seem more like the "let's cross our fingers" type.

Generally, weddings bore me. It's kind of like watching the same play over and over and over, just with different actors. I go to weddings because I care about at least one of the people getting married, but I'm usually also trying to figure out a way to spend the least amount of time there as is appropriate. But it's a little different when my middle-aged friends get married: the wedding is still boring, but I'm happier for them. They had all managed to build pretty nice lives for themselves while single, so they weren't getting married because they needed help getting set on life's path. Their new spouses were chosen for all the ways they could enhance their lives, not because they were needed to help construct the life.

And, even better, these new spouses have also enhanced my life. I feel like I've gained a bunch of new friends. I really like these guys. Although they've been useless in terms of introducing me to their single friends, I forgive them.

Guys don't like getting mixed up in match-making. For example, a woman I used to know introduced me to her new husband's cousin and it didn't go well at all. Within 5 minutes of meeting him, I knew that this wouldn't be any fun. He had cornrows and I hated his clothes (shirt and pants that matched like a small child's outfit), and he walked like he was looking for a fight. I think he thought I was a snob. Unfortunately, my friend and her husband had planned a whole day for the four of us. Awkward. The day felt two days long as we went from lunch at their house in New Jersey to the beach, stopping at a local fair on the way, and then on to dinner. I don't think anybody really had any fun that day. I think the only thing "my date" and I had in common was that we both knew the couple and we both were single. He had to know that nothing was going to come of this, and I honestly believe that he was no more interested in me than I was in him. But, being a man, I guess he figured he would try to see what he could get out of it, so he made a pass at me anyway. (Sigh). My friend and her brand new husband were a little annoyed with me for a while after that because by the end of the evening I had stopped pretending that I was having a good time. So maybe all my friends' new husbands know what they're doing by just staying out of it. That's where they draw the line in our new-found friendship.

Here's another issue. When my friends get married, it makes more work for me. It is good for me to have a multitude of people I enjoy and who I can call on to socialize with in any number of ways, and I'm now down by four. Their time is being taken up by their husbands (and child, in a couple of cases), so they have neither the time nor the inclination to come out and play with me in the same way as often as I would like. If I call them up and say "meet me in an hour for a drink," the answer is likely to be some version of "no." Even worse, a couple of them even had the audacity to move to another city with their new husbands. So our outings now require more forethought.

Many thanks to my single friends for remaining in the sisterhood with me! (You know who you are). I need someone to come out and play with me.

And many thanks to my newly–married girlfriends for bringing their guys into my life.

See? Two for the price of one.

[9] Rethinking the Marriage Crunch, *Newsweek*, June 5, 2006

LESSON 15

Go to therapy if you're crazy.

It's not some cute personality quirk. If it's getting in the way, do something about it. This is actually good advice for everybody, whether married or not. I wish I had done it 20 years earlier.

Ibelieve that in every relationship, one person is Ike Turner and the other is Tina; that is, one is a fool and the other accommodates the fool. While I know this isn't true in every relationship, but I do think it's true in most. And in some relationships, both people are Ike... two fools together. I was in one of those relationships, at least once.

I met Tommy (not his real name) many years ago at a popular hang-out in Washington, DC, my hometown. I was living in NYC at the time, but came home fairly regularly to visit my family and see my friends. One Friday night, I went with some girlfriends to Hogate's, a restaurant and bar on the Potomac River. It had a nice view and was a fun place to drink, dance, and meet up with old and new friends. I ran into a guy I knew from high school and Tommy was with him. We talked, flirted, and exchanged phone numbers. He was from New York, now living in DC. His family was still in New York and mine was in DC, so we had ample excuses to find ourselves in the other's town. We started dating.

I was a lot crazier then than I am now. I had a pretty strong personality and was stubborn. I could go to ridiculous lengths to prove a point. The expression I believe is: cut off your nose to spite your face (something my mother would often accuse me of). Tommy, too, had a strong personality and was stubborn. He, too, could go to ridiculous lengths to prove a point. We were both Ike Turner.

He was controlling; I was not to be controlled. Once, he made fun of me for wearing tan shoes with a black outfit.

I made sure to wear tan shoes with a different black outfit the next time I saw him. He used to tell me that he was going to "break me," tame me, make me more accommodating. A woman with good sense would have taken that as a sign to move on, but I was not that woman. I dug in. "You can't break me."

A few months into the relationship, I went to DC to visit him for a few days. I arrived on a Sunday and we had our usual evening–some fighting and some making up. I don't remember what Sunday night's fight was about, but it must have been a good one. When he left for work on Monday, he still had an attitude. I knew he was up to something by his swagger, but I didn't know what. I found out pretty quickly. The doors to his house had locks that required keys to open them from the inside. As he was leaving for work, he took the inside keys with him. That MF locked me in his apartment! And he was going to be gone all day. I was trapped.

I thought, "Okay, now I know he's really crazy. I'm actually locked in this place with no way of getting out. This is super crazy." However, stubborn jackass that I was, there was no way I was going to call and plead with him to let me out. I was not going to let him win. I considered breaking a window. It would serve him right. I thought about calling the police, but I was afraid it could get ugly and they would kill him. So I did neither. Plus, breaking a window or calling the police would have told him that I was scared, and that I couldn't handle it. And he would've won...and that wasn't going to happen. Besides, I wasn't scared, I was pissed. It did occur to me that I would be in big trouble if a fire broke out, but I figured I could break the window then.

If he thought this would break me, he was very wrong. I settled in. I lay on the couch and read the newspaper. I thought about going for a run, then I remembered I couldn't get out. So I found an exercise channel on TV and worked out with Margaret on Body Electric. I made breakfast. Shit, there was no milk for coffee, and I couldn't get to the store to buy milk. So, I didn't have coffee. Then I spent a couple of hours on the phone catching up with friends. I told no one about my situation. By then, it was midday and the day actually hadn't been so bad. If I had forgotten that I was locked in and couldn't get out, it would have just felt like any other relaxing and lazy day. I read a book I brought with me. At one point, I thought about visiting a girlfriend…before I remembered I couldn't get out. The lunch I made from dinner leftovers was nice and leisurely because I had nowhere to go. Then I took a nap.

I was sprawled on the bed watching television when he came home. I'm sure he expected to find me in tears or some state of anxiety. He really didn't know me. I looked up at him, smiled, asked him how his day was. I told him: "My day was great, quiet and relaxing." I acted like I didn't even know I'd been locked in. He said nothing about it. Neither did I.

Now this is how you know I was really crazy. Whenever I tell this story, most people ask me how long afterward I ended the relationship: That day? The next day? As soon as I returned home to NYC? Nope. Nope. And nope. Tommy and I dated for three more years. Break me? Was he kidding? My attitude was "bring it on" (which, of course, is ridiculous).

Don't stay in a crazy relationship.

LESSON 16

You can't force chemistry.

If it's not there, move on.   I believe that I know, pretty much on sight, whether or not a guy is for me.   I'm usually not wrong.   Still, every now and then I would meet a guy in whom I had zero interest, but would go out with him because he seemed nice (or something else equally trite).   I would think that if I just spent more time with him, he'd grow on me and all would be fine. Never happened.

I prefer to tell stories where the male is the bad guy, but in this one, it might be me. I didn't plan it that way; it just kind of happened. Shortly before my 35th birthday, I met a guy at the bar of a restaurant in Soho. I was meeting some friends for dinner and got there early. I've been known to sometimes show up a bit early to have a drink at the bar and scope out the "merchandise." Sometimes my efforts are fruitful, sometimes not. This time they were. He was tall the way I like them, mustachioed the way I like them, and eager to pay for my drink...which I also like. Our conversation was light-hearted and easy. By the time my friends showed up, we'd exchanged telephone numbers and made plans for dinner in a few days. I felt like I'd scored again, yet at the same time I had a little bit of a nagging doubt. He seemed a little too self-conscious and unsure of himself in a way I found unappealing. He was also a little too self-deprecating. I thought I should overlook these shortcomings because he seemed like a nice guy who was also pretty interesting.

Dinner a few days later was good. We went to the 21 Club where he was well-known by the staff. We had a long dinner, talking late into the night, and then took a long walk before he put me in a cab for home. He was clearly smitten with me, and a little further along in that way than I was. I had a nice time, though still had that same nagging feeling: he was a smart man who had had quite a bit of success in real estate, so I didn't understand why he seemed so insecure.

On our fourth date, he offered to take me to Paris for my upcoming birthday. I admit that I knew that this was prob-

ably extreme: we didn't know each other like that and I
didn't really like him like that. Nevertheless, I didn't have
big plans for my birthday and I thought a trip to Paris was
always a fine idea. Plus, it was free. Who was I to deprive
him of this opportunity? My birthday was more than a
month away. I had plenty of time to grow fonder of him.

Two days before my birthday, we boarded a flight to Paris.
I admit to being disappointed that we were flying coach.
Really? It was my birthday. Plus, he's a regular at the 21
Club and had a place in Easthampton. (It was a condo, but
still…). Why were we flying coach? I didn't say anything
because I didn't want to seem ungrateful, but I was feeling a
little like a brat. I was mean to the old lady behind me who
thought I'd taken her magazine. "They printed more than
one copy of this magazine, you know." I could have just
told her that this was mine and I didn't know what happened to hers, but I was on a transatlantic flight in coach
and couldn't get comfortable, dammit.

Don (not his real name) and I talked most of the flight
about all kinds of things, getting to know each other even
better. By the time we landed, I knew that this trip was
not a good idea. I wasn't feeling attracted to him the way I
should. I hid it, or so I thought. In customs, we ran into
a guy I used to work for many years before. I went over
to say hello to him and his family. I forgot to bring Don
with me. My ex-employer asked me: who's this guy you're
with? His tone suggested something was amiss. I told him
we were going to Paris for my birthday. "He's not the guy
for you…and you know it." Whoa. That really threw me:
he was right but, damn, was it that obvious? I denied that

what he said was true. I felt embarrassed.

When we got to the hotel, there had been a mix-up, and the only rooms available had two twin beds. Don was upset. The French lady at the desk was unmoved. There was nothing they could do. I was relieved. I couldn't imagine how I was going to sleep with this man–this nice man who had done nothing wrong, and who was treating me to Paris for my birthday. I had zero attraction to him. It was going to be a long week.

The first night was easy. We went to an early dinner near the hotel, had a bottle of wine, then collapsed into our respective beds because we were both exhausted. The twin beds didn't matter. We just wanted to sleep. He did try to push them together but it didn't work. They were either too heavy or maybe bolted somehow to something because we couldn't budge them…thank God.

Each day, we got up, had a cute, tiny French breakfast and coffee, then headed out to enjoy this beautiful city. The days were lovely. At night, I was an ass. I had to continually come up with creative ways to avoid the romance thing: "jet lag is killing me." It even gave me a really bad headache. The next night, I pretended to have menstrual cramps. Certainly no one could expect me to have sex when I didn't feel well. Those darn cramps lasted two days, and they were always worse at night. Then I pretended I had actually gotten my period. I told him I wasn't comfortable having sex when I was bleeding; surely he could understand. Of course he did, but couldn't I just cuddle with him a bit? Well surely I could do that; I didn't dislike him, I just wasn't drawn to him in that way. By night five, he asked how long my periods last. A week to ten days I said. He was sad. And thank goodness he wasn't the confident, take-charge kind of guy I prefer. It might have been harder to pull off this stunt. (On the other hand, I might not have needed to because he'd be the kind of guy I'd want to do these things with). The next night he got a little more forward. Could I kiss him a bit, maybe hold him while he, ummm…made himself happy? Okay, I figured a week-long, all-expenses paid trip to Paris was at least worth that…so I did. Plus, I was happy that he didn't expect me to do it for him. Fortunately, we left the next day; I don't think I would have had the stomach for another night of that.

The entire flight home, he talked about how much more wonderful the trip would have been if we had been able to "do it" with the city of Paris as our backdrop. I agreed that would have been lovely, indeed, but what could we do when Mother Nature interfered? We saw each other once more; I told him that I'd reconciled with my ex. I do feel bad about this one. But there's no forcing chemistry, right?

LESSON 17

**If you have to think about it,
you don't really want a baby.**

Don't even go there. It's too important a decision. It's
not like you can change your mind later.

Y ou've probably noticed that "I've never really wanted kids" has been a theme with me…except for a couple of weeks when I was turning 40 and I became psychotic. Here's what happened. I received a phone call from one of my favorite guys of all times. We had dated off-and-on for quite a few years. He had loved me, almost from the beginning, and I loved him, too. He was steady like a rock. I was erratic and restless, and would break off the relationship on a whim. Still, I always found my way back to him, and he always took me in. He eventually got tired of me not marrying him, though, so he finally married someone else --someone he described as "having been nicer to him than anyone ever had," which might have been a bit of a dig at me.

But he called me on this day to make a proposal of a different kind: we should have a baby, me and him. I cracked up at the absurdity…at first. I was also pretty surprised. We were both aware of two truths: he was married, and I didn't want a kid. That should have ended it right there because what was there to discuss? It turns out, there was more to discuss. His general nature was to be a deliberate and clear thinker, so I listened.

He explained that he really wanted to have a child with me as a way to keep us connected. We were soul mates, after all. For a reason I still don't understand, instead of just stopping the conversation right there, I laid out all the reasons why this couldn't happen. He had a counter-point for each one.

Me: "I don't really want a kid."

Him: "You'll want ours. He'll have the best of both of us. It'll be great."

Me: "I can't afford a kid."

Him: "I'll help you. I'll give you $10,000 a month child support."

Me: "But my work has me traveling too much."

Him: "You can have a live-in nanny. Take her with you."

Me: "My apartment is too small."

Him: "So we'll have to find you something bigger."

And that's when I started getting excited. Wow! An apartment in New York City, large enough for me, my kid, and the nanny? Plus, it'd have to have a guest bedroom for my family and friends who I could now encourage to visit often. My very own four-bedroom apartment in Manhattan! Actually, I think I preferred a loft. That would be so cool!

So that's how my bout with psychosis began. This was perfect. Having a child immediately became much more attractive when the package included enough money to make it really manageable (on top of what I already earned), a big, fabulous apartment and–most importantly–someone else to mostly raise the kid for me. Not a bad deal at all. I spent the next few days excitedly thinking about what neighborhood I would choose for my new apartment:

would I stay in Chelsea or move to Soho? The Upper East Side was out–not my style. If I stayed in Chelsea, which I really loved, maybe we could buy the apartments on either side of me and just knock down the walls. I wondered if my neighbors would sell at a good price. I also like Tribeca a lot, and started focusing my efforts there because I'd seen a lot of great lofts there. I started looking online to see what was available and at what price point. There was a lot of good-looking real estate in Tribeca. This was so much fun. I had to remember to ask him how much money we had to work with.

I quickly realized that another good thing about this little arrangement was that I could work less, if I wanted. I was self-employed as a consultant in the marketing business. Business was good and I liked it well enough, but I would have been happy to work less. This arrangement would allow me to do that without compromising my lifestyle. Life was about to get even better. I figured I'd work part-time for a year or so after the baby was born, getting back in shape, and maybe traveling a bit. There were just a few more issues he and I needed to discuss, though.

When we spoke again, I mentioned that we would do this through artificial insemination. Illogically, I could have a baby with a married man, but I couldn't have sex with one. That would just be wrong. He wasn't happy to hear that. I pointed out that a little medical help would increase the likelihood of pregnancy, especially at my advanced age. We went round and round on that one for a while, and he finally relented. I think. What I think actually happened is he said we'd discuss it later.

So then I asked how he would explain our child to his mother. He and his mom were close. I assumed he wouldn't tell his wife, but surely his mom would want to know she had another grandchild. That's when he started stuttering. He had been unbelievably smooth during all our conversations, until now. He had obviously given this a lot of thought and was sure that this was what he wanted to do and how we wanted to do it, so I was a little taken aback when he said "Oh, she can't know. We have to keep this quiet." What? So, I said I thought it would be unfair for my darling, sweet kid to be denied knowing his grandmother. My mom had been dead for years, so his was the only option for my kid to know a grandmother's love. But Boyfriend was steadfast on this one. He was clearly more worried about his mother than his wife. And keeping it quiet meant that people would obviously know I had a kid but I couldn't tell anyone who I'd had the kid with. So, let me get this straight: I'm going to have a child but no one can know who the father is? How was that supposed to work? And what would I tell him? (It was always "him"). And that's when everything came to a screeching halt. No way could I do this. Not like this with that condition.

In a metaphorical blink of an eye, I went from being giddy with excitement at my new impending life—to—being dropped back to reality with a great, big thud. Darn. I wasn't going to get that big, fancy downtown loft after all. Nor the baby, thank goodness, because I knew I didn't really want one.

LESSON 18

Accept help when it's offered.

Don't be stupid. Being independent doesn't mean you can't let someone help you...especially when you need it.

About six months after I moved to New York, I realized that I needed to sell my car. It was a red Honda Accord, the only car I've owned that wasn't a convertible. It was a little corny, but it had safely taken me on many rides, even moving me here from Washington, DC. I was living on 42nd Street and 8th Avenue (yep!), and long-term, on-street parking was practically non-existent. I couldn't afford to garage my car on a daily basis, so selling was really my only option.

I was dating a guy who lived in the Bronx who kindly offered to let me park my car at his place-a super-large apartment complex with seemingly thousands of parking spaces -until the car was sold. I placed an ad in the newspaper and immediately received lots of calls. This would be easy, I thought. Never having sold a car before, I had no idea how many people would call, say they were interested, and then never call again. It was really frustrating. One guy made me cry when he pulled out of the deal at the zero hour. He had come to see the car-twice-called a couple of times to make sure it was still available while he got his money together, and haggled with me until we reached a price we could both live with. About an hour before he was to pick up the car and deliver the much-needed check, he called to say he'd changed his mind. Ugh.

The next day, though, I received a call that was really promising. A very nice young man was interested and thought the price sounded fair, so we made arrangements for him to see the car the next day. I took the day off from work and went to hang out at my boyfriend's, Barry's (not his real name) apartment until the interested buyer showed up.

When the phone rang, I agreed to meet the buyer in the lot where the car was parked. Barry insisted on coming down with me, and I stubbornly refused. It wasn't necessary, and I didn't need any help. I was an independent woman. He should just wait in the apartment until I got back, and then we'd go get a bite to eat. (You know this was a long time ago because, these days, I would've tried to convince him to go down, while I hung out in the apartment!)

When I got to my car, I was greeted by two guys: the buyer and someone he introduced as his brother. He hadn't mentioned that he was bringing anyone, but what did it matter? They seemed nice enough and I needed to sell my car. We talked about the car a bit and then we all sat in it, checking out the inside. I was in the passenger seat, and the brother in the backseat.

"How about taking it for a spin around the lot?" the potential buyer said.

"Sure, why not," I responded, handing him the keys. Bad move. Shortly after he started the car, he showed me the gun that was now in his right hand. I still remember the absurdity of the next words we spoke.

"You know what this is, don't you," he asked.

I swallowed and said, "Yes, of course." I stupidly thought he was asking whether I recognized that the item in his hand was a gun, but he actually meant much more. He was asking if I recognized the whole situation for what it was. I then saw another gun in the hand of our backseat passenger. This was not at all the way I had expected this deal to go.

He drove us out of the parking lot and onto the highway. He was driving. Much of what happened next was a blur. They drove me around for I-have-no-idea-how-long; it could've been twenty minutes, could've been two hours and twenty minutes. The driver had rested his gun on his lap, but the guy in the backseat kept his aimed at me the entire time. He was seated behind the driver and pointed the gun through the opening between the two front seats. I remember talking constantly but have no memory (then or now) of what I said. I was sure Barry was wondering what was taking so long. Cellphones hadn't really been invented yet, so there was no way to call and let him know that I was going to be late…if I was coming back at all. As we drove by a wooded area that seemed like a good place to dump a body, I remember thinking that I had never told my family about my tattoo. If someone called and said they'd found the body of a woman who fits the description of your loved one and she has a tattoo, my family would have said "that's not her," so my body would have remained unclaimed in the morgue forever. I made a note to myself that if I got out of this alive, I should let my family know about the picture of the cute bitten apple I'd recently acquired.

After driving me around awhile, they seemed to be unsure what to do next, so I took this as an opportunity. I suggested they let me out, take the car and my purse, and we'd just forget about it. I was surprised that they actually agreed. (Why didn't I think of this earlier?) They even let me have my house keys, but they wanted my gold chain.

I let them have it but convinced them to let me keep the pearls. They agreed, apparently having no use for or understanding of pearls (including that the pearls were worth hundreds of dollars more than the gold chain). Worse, the pearls weren't even mine. My sister's friend, Faye, had loaned them to me as a one-year moving-to-New York gift. It wouldn't have been good not to be able to return Faye's pearls to her when the year was up.

The buyer and his brother let me out on some street in the Bronx and drove off. Having no idea where I was, I walked a few blocks and finally asked someone where I could find a police officer. I was directed to the Bronx Courthouse a few blocks away. I calmly walked over there and told the clerk I'd been robbed and kidnapped and needed to speak to someone. She actually didn't believe me because I was so calm. I was directed to sit in the waiting room.

Two cops eventually came in and called my name. As soon as I saw them, my calm façade disappeared and I burst into tears. It was as if seeing the cops made it all real. After I calmed down, I gave them the report, trying to answer their questions with as much detail as I could recall (which was almost none at all). They seemed bored. In fact, I was offended that one of the officers worked on a crossword puzzle the whole time. I understood that this was pretty routine for them, but a little compassion wouldn't have hurt. Afterward, they dropped me at the subway to go home. I didn't have money for a subway token (I had just been robbed), so one of the cops gave me the money. I didn't think to ask if I could call Barry to let him know I was okay or what was taking so long. I called him as soon as I got home. He yelled at me and was kind enough to point out to me, repeatedly, that I should have let him come with me when I went to meet the buyer. I hung up, exhausted, collapsed into bed, and slept hard. As I was drifting off, I made the decision at that moment that New York would be my new permanent home. Though I had initially planned to stay only for a year, I was now a statistic…on the books…and I felt that made me a New Yorker. I was home.

A few days later, I got a call from the cops. They found the guys, still driving around in my car, my purse in the trunk, which made it kind of easy to prove the case. They were both 17 years old, though I had described them as being about 30. I guess the guns made them look much older. We went to court and they were given 3-5 years. They'd done this before.

Here's the moral to this story: if I hadn't been so insistent on not getting married, none of this would have happened. My husband would have handled the car sale for me.

At the very least, I should have accepted Barry's help.

LESSON **19**

Wear high heels.

High heels are sexy. You look sexy to men and, perhaps more importantly, you feel sexy. That is, of course, if your feet don't hurt.

I don't have a story to go with this one…just an observation: I get a lot more attention from guys when I'm wearing heels than when I'm not. That's not really a surprise, but it happens way more now that I'm old(ish). Many years ago, all I needed was my youth to catch a man's eye. Now that that's gone, it takes props. That's okay. I love wearing heels. The thing is, heels look good but they don't always feel good, and therein lies the problem. There comes a time in a woman's life when comfort and practicality start to just make more sense. Many of the items we wore in the name of fashion when we were young eventually start to seem a little foolish: my Daisy Duke shorts (that a few of my girlfriends threatened to burn if I didn't stop wearing them…well into my 40s), leg warmers, my black velvet cat suit, my first fur: a cute little jacket in white rabbit. When I was wearing any of them, you couldn't tell me I wasn't fly, but there did come a time when they became ridiculous. You see, fashion changes, but the allure of heels does not. And though most high heels, on a long day are neither comfortable nor practical, that's not the point.

You don't have to wear high heels every day, but I think it's important not to give up on them. If you want to meet a man, heels are one of your easiest and best tools. Guys are visual. They like the way a woman looks and walks in heels. Plus, if you can walk in them, you look and feel differently, too: cuter, sexier, more alive. The key, though, is "if you can walk in them." One of my pet peeves is a woman clunking along in heels that she can't walk in. You want to look captivating, not like a doofus. If your feet hurt or you just haven't mastered the art of doing your thing in heels, hold off until you're ready. But do get ready.

What's key is that you don't lose sight of yourself as a sexual being, even if you're not seeing anyone right now. You will be: throw on some heels, strut your stuff, and get your mojo working! Watch how many eyes you catch...

LESSON 20

Being single and childfree is good.

There's a lot to be said for being single and childfree.
Revel in it. (Lots of people wish they had it like that).

I am not anti-husband. There are a lot of good reasons to have one, many of which I've outlined elsewhere. I'm not anti-kid, either. There are also a few good reasons to have them… like you can always use them as an excuse to get out of anything you don't want to do ("Sorry, I can't. Annie's allergic…or has a toothache…or a soccer game…"). But there are also an awful lot of good things about being single, no husband, no kids…just me and the dog. Some of my favorites include:

- I often get a " pass" because people think I'm odd. When you don't have a husband or a child…and you could, but chose not to, there's obviously something wrong with you. This works in my favor all kinds of ways because people expect less of me. I know that my social skills can be a bit awkward. Some people think I'm unfriendly. What most people who know me don't know is that I'm actually shy. I work hard to mask it, which often causes clumsy encounters because it's hard to mask who you are. I once took a personality test that described me as "an introvert masquerading as an extrovert." I think that sums it up quite nicely. Interestingly, I once overheard someone explaining my behavior by saying, "you know, she's never been married." So, instead of having to admit to awkwardly trying to hide my shyness, I can blame my behavior on my un-husbanded status.

- Being free of husband and child(ren) also allows me to get away with things that most responsible adults cannot, like not having much food in my refrigerator, not having an ironing board, and using the same pots I bought when I graduated from college. I realize this sounds a little like a prolonged adolescence… without the acne or curfew that usually comes with being a teen. Another advantage: it keeps me young.

- Because I don't have a family of my own, I get invited to many events for the holidays. I feel very lucky on Thanksgiving, Easter, Independence Day, and every holiday that's celebrated with a family gathering. I love the invitations. I know that I get them sometimes because the hosts feel sorry for me, but I don't care.

- Travel is one of my passions. Honestly, I mostly work so I can fund my next trip. I've traveled throughout the U.S. to major cities and small towns, plus Argentina, Brazil, the Caribbean, China, Costa Rica, England, France, Hungary, Indonesia, Ireland, Spain, South Africa, Switzerland, Tanzania, and United Arab Emirates. I want to go everywhere, and I pretty much can because my time and my money are my own. I spend my dollars however I want without having to consider if it could be better spent on my child's braces or my husband's birthday party.

- I can give my callers my undivided attention. Talking to me on the phone should be a real pleasure, because you're the only person I'm talking to the whole time. I don't ("Stop it, Billy"), continually interrupt the conversation ("No, I haven't seen your keys") to speak to other people in the house ("Don't you look pretty, sweetheart"), usually without even bothering to say "excuse me" or "I'm sorry." You're the only person I'm talking to. I sure wish the reverse were true.

- Firm(ish) tits, and no stretch marks.

- I can date whoever I want...without having to worry about his effect on my kids. If I had kids, I would have to make more responsible choices in the men I bring home. He would have to have good manners and not curse too much. He'd have to watch his alcohol intake. He would have to like other people's kids and act interested in them. He couldn't spend the night in my bed or walk around my house in his boxer shorts. He would have to be gainfully employed. Fortunately, I don't have to think about these kinds of things when I'm assessing my next guy.

- I don't know what it's like to have to regularly have sex that I don't really feel like having. When we reach that point in the relationship, I'm usually gone.

- If I had kids and he had kids, things could get complicated. We'd have to plan our dates around lots of schedules: my kids' and his kids' schedules, my kids' father's and his kids' mother's schedule. Imagine having concert tickets and having to figure all this out. Just thinking about it gives me a headache. Fortunately, this won't be a problem for me.

- In 1998, I quit my job because I decided I wanted to work for myself. (Actually I didn't want to work at all, but I couldn't quite figure out how to make that happen). I thought about it seriously for only a couple of weeks, and didn't have a business plan or a client. It didn't matter, though, because I was tired of being expected to show up at the office every day at 9 a.m. Suppose I didn't feel like showing up until 11:30 a.m.? Clearly the answer was to make my own hours. I can only imagine, though, what would have happened if I had come home from work one day and announced to the family that I was going to quit my job and do my own thing…with no real plan. It might not have been received so well. I loved the idea, though, and I was the only one who mattered.

- One of the most helpful things about still being single? My sense of humor is continually sharpened as I must constantly come up with clever ways to deflect the same tiresome questions: Why aren't you married? You don't have any kids? Who's gonna take care of you when you're old? Ad nauseum…

But don't just take my word for it. I asked a few girl-friends to weigh in on what they love about being single and childfree. In a nutshell, there's a real sense of freedom, plus some other perks:

Nicky said:
- I don't have to account for my whereabouts.

- No one bugs me about anything, which enables me to concentrate 100% on my business.

- I don't have to be unnecessarily social since many couples don't want single folks hanging around, which is nice. This cuts down on buying tickets to events and attending parties I don't really want to be bothered with.

- My money can go toward my passion for handbags and shoes, and no one asks "is that new?" There are no stupid questions and no lying.

- I can stay on the phone all day with my girl-friends, if I choose.

Heather said:
- I can be the favorite or cool aunt, the one who gives a kid undivided attention, the things they want vs need, and knows the latest music and movies.

- I can travel at a moment's notice anywhere I want
.

- It can truly be "all about me"

Darlene said:
- I have total freedom in all areas of life. After a long day of being a professional at work, I don't need to be a short order cook, maid, disciplinarian, etc. at night

Phyllis said:
- I like my solitude. Once I am home and close the door, I know I control my peace and quiet.

- I like not having to be responsible for another person or having others depend on me all the time.

- I can come and go when I please and not have to consider someone else or their schedule when I plan mine.

Colleen said:
- The only person I have to clean up after is myself!

- I can clean my kitchen in the buff. Can't do that with kids around!

- I can hang out with the girls whenever I want to and not hear him complain!

Karen said:
- I don't have to feel guilty about buying the lat-

est YSL or Gucci bag versus saving for the college fund!

Michelle said:

- I can have white carpet in every room of my house and not worry about it getting dirty.

- Doing what I want, when I want and not having to consider someone else's space because it is all my space.

Maureen said:

- I can sleep in peace and quiet, no snoring.

- Control of the thermostat and remote are all mine.

- I can watch whatever I want on TV and never have to see a sports game.

- I can work out when it fits my schedule and not worry about picking up the kids or having dinner ready at a certain hour.

- My boobs haven't dropped to my waist, as I've never borne a child and breast fed.

Lucy said:

- I open the fridge and the things in there are the things I bought earlier

Just so you know, this is not sour grapes. These women

date and some are in relationships. Nobody's saying that she wouldn't appreciate sharing her space and her life—long term—with a special someone, but there is definitely an upside to being accountable to no one but yourself!

"Until the advent of feminism,
Spinsterhood was generally
portrayed as a condition to be
pitied or mocked."

(Reference.com www.reference.com/browse/Spinster?jss=0)

For some, it still is. But we're changing that.
We're Spinsterlicious, baby!
–Eleanore Wells

APPENDIX

Just the Facts, Ma'am

"Unmarried women played a pivotal role in making history and in changing this nation. Barack Obama would have lost the women's vote and the 2008 election if it were not for the contribution of unmarried women. All told, he split men 49–48 percent, but lost married women 47–50 percent. Unmarried women, however, delivered 70 percent of their vote to the Democratic candidate, up from 62 percent in 2004."

(*Unmarried women play critical role in historic election.* Greenberg Quinlan Rosner Research Women's Voices. Women Vote November, 2008).

THE SPINSTERS HALL OF FAME

Fabulous Spinsters
Real and Make-believe*

- Auntie Mame*
- Bessie Delany
- Bridget Jones*
- Cameron Diaz
- Chelsea Handler
- Clara Barton
- Coco Chanel
- Condoleeza Rice
- Darryl Hannah
- Debbie Harry
- Dorothy Height
- Dorothy West
- Elaine Benes*
- Elena Kagan
- Emily Bronte
- Emily Dickinson
- Eudora Welty
- Florence Nightingale
- Greta Garbo
- Harper Lee
- Helen Keller
- Helene Cooper
- Jacqueline Bisset
- Jane Austen
- Jane Goodall
- Jane Marple*
- Janet Napolitano
- Janet Reno
- Janis Joplin
- Jessye Norman
- Joan of Arc
- Lizzie Borden
- Mae Jemison
- Mary Poppins*
- Mary Richards *
- Maureen Dowd
- Mellody Hobson
- Miss Piggy*
- Mother Teresa
- Naomi Campbell
- Oprah Winfrey
- Pam Grier
- Patricia Clarkson
- Patti Austin
- Robin Roberts
- Rosie Perez
- Sanaa Lathan
- Sarah Delany
- Susan B. Anthony
- Suzanne Malveaux
- Tracee Ellis Ross
- Tyra Banks

QUOTABLE QUOTES:
On Having Children

Always be nice to your children because they are the ones who will choose your rest home.
-Phyllis Diller-

Children nowadays are tyrants. They contradict their parents, gobble their food and tyrannise their teachers.
-Socrates-

When my husband comes home, if the kids are still alive, I figure I've done my job.
-Roseanne Barr-

I like children… Properly cooked.
-WC Fields-

Insanity is hereditary: You can get it from your children.
-Sam Levinson-

Raising kids is part joy and part guerilla warfare.
-Ed Asner-

QUOTABLE QUOTES:
On Being Single

Why get married and make one man miserable when I can stay single and make thousands miserable?
-Carrie Snow-

I'm just an old maid… who likes men.
-Janet Reno-

A woman without a man is like a fish without a bicycle.
-Gloria Steinem-

Marriage is a great institution, but I'm not ready for an institution yet.
-Mae West-

Couples should live close, and visit often.
-Mae West-

When a girl marries she exchanges the attentions of many men for the inattention of one.
-Helen Rowland-

The poor wish to be rich, the rich wish to be happy, the single wish to be married, and the married wish to be dead.
-Ann Landers-

What a lovely surprise to finally discover how unlonely being alone can be.
-Ellen Burstyn-

About The Author

Born and raised in Washington, DC, Eleanore Wells now lives in and loves New York City. When she's not blogging about "the single life" (www.TheSpinsterliciousLife.com), she's running her own consumer research and strategy firm, Golden Door Consulting.

12178397R00076

Made in the USA
Charleston, SC
18 April 2012